The Age of Intelligence

A Call for A Radical Change in Our Way of Thinking and Acting

Vaasamoorti

COPYRIGHT

Copyright © 2019 by Vaasamoorti.

www.vaasamoorti.com

The Age of Intellingence/Vaasamoorti —2nd ed.

KDP ISBN 9798840744550

Contact the Author

Contact Vaasamoorti

If you would like to discuss the ideas in this book feel free to email the author Vaasamoorti@yahoo.com

ACKNOWLEDGEMENTS

I would like to thank Sheryl Kennedy Coe for bringing the team together that made publishing this e-book possible. I would also like to thank her for setting up my website and proofreading the manuscript.

I would like to thank Thomas Bennett Jr. for his work in formatting this book for electronic distribution, as well as the fine job he did editing the manuscript.

CONTENTS

PREFACE

As a boy of fifteen I happened to read Citizen Tom Paine's two famous books: *Common Sense* and *The Age of Reason.* As a British subject he believed strongly that the American colonies should be independent and he argued vigorously that the colonists should fight for their freedom. His powerful advocacy made a great impression on my young mind, as it was the time of the freedom movement in India and independence from the United Kingdom was still far in the future.

It was *The Age of Reason* that left some uneasiness in me that lasted for several years. As my studies advanced I came to realize that **"Reason"** was not enough to make the world a better place. We see that despite the presence of so many great and brilliant intellectuals, who can analyze any situation and offer solutions, mankind continues to wallow in multifarious problems. Poverty, hunger, disease and despair stalk the land. Yet man hates man and fights him. Mass murders and genocide are quite common. The reason is **"Reason"** is only one faculty of man and does not touch his entire personality. It is **intelligence** as envisaged in the following pages, that takes man's physical and spiritual needs, his desires, dreams, beliefs, sentiments, emotions and all into its grasp. It is through intelligence that we may build a safer and happier world. That is, in quintessence, the approach of this book. I do not expect all readers to agree with me, but if they are patient enough to listen fully to what I have to say and judge for themselves, that will be enough for me.

Vaasamoorti

I: Introductory

A wild and impossible dream of man for ages, landing on the moon, was realized in 1969. Man is now almost ready to venture forth to the worlds beyond. But the word 'man' should not mislead us. The moon is not within the reach of everybody. Only half a dozen men have so far landed on the moon. Their number is not likely to go up in the near future. The landing on the moon is only symbolical of the magnitude and potentiality of man's achievements. Once again the use of 'man' here is misleading. It is our science and technology that dominate our world today. Think of all the inventions of science and technology: motor cars, railway trains, steamers, airplanes, telegraph, telephone, cinema, radio, television, modern factories producing millions of various articles required by man, the revolutionary discoveries of medicines, the taming of rivers, the use of electricity, the splitting of the atom and the exploitation of the unlimited nuclear energy, the electronics revolution, computers and, the most important of all for the existence of man—the developments in agricultural science. Truly science and technology are now at such a stage that they can provide every man, woman, and child with all the necessaries and comforts of life, so that there need be no more hunger, malnutrition, disease and poverty, and each and every one can enjoy life commensurate to the status of man in the order of evolution. Indeed one is amazed at the possibilities and potentialities of science and technology.

But let us not be carried away by the possibilities and potentialities of science and technology. Let us face the harsh realities.

Let us see what we have actually been doing with the same science and technology. We come to the costliest 'hobby' of mankind, war and all that it involves. Then we shall realize the full extent of the great tragedy that humanity faces today.

It was said that with the money spent on the First World War a school and a hospital could have been opened in every town and village in the world, and a small, but handsome, cash gift could have been given to every man and woman alive.[1] This was only the money cost of the war. But also think of the millions of people killed, not only soldiers, but also ordinary men, women and children far away from the battlefield, the hundreds and thousands of families disrupted, and the thousands of villages, towns and cities destroyed. A little more than eleven million were estimated killed during that War.

If you come to the Second World War you will learn that it was several times more costly than the first one, both in terms of human life and material resources.[2] The erstwhile Soviet Union alone lost more than twenty five million people, that is, about twelve percent of her population in that War. Tens of thousands of people living in the cities of Hiroshima and Nagasaki were killed in a matter of seconds by the first two atom bombs. (The Hiroshima bomb was said to be 2000 times more powerful than the largest conventional bomb then in existence—20,000 tons each. Estimates of deaths during the Second World War vary from 50 to 72 million.

We have traveled far from the days of the Second World War. Now there are nuclear weapons which are several times more powerful than the first two atom bombs that destroyed Hiroshima and Nagasaki. There are besides, the other kind of bombs, biological and chemical weapons, the Inter Continental Ballistic Missiles (The ICBMs) the Multiple Independently Targetable Reentry Vehicles the MIRVs), jet fighters and bombers, warships, destroyers, aircraft carriers, the submarines (nuclear or otherwise), tanks, guns and all such machines of death and destruction. We must also consider the hundreds of ordnance factories, the armies of workers, technicians, engineers, managers and administrative staff required to run them, and the thousands of scientists and technologists whose intelligence is directed towards improving the existing weapons and inventing newer and more destructive ones. And finally, there is the cost of keeping millions under arms. Let us take a small example : A nuclear submarine is said to cost $900 million. a jet bomber $15 million and a missile $75 million. Think of how many nuclear submarines there are, similarly how many bombers, how many missiles there are. According to one authority the annual expenditure on the war machine until recently all over the world was around 7,500 billion dollars.

It is no wonder that 'defense' is said to take the lion's share of a nation's budget while many urgently needed social welfare schemes go abegging for funds. In this connection a few quotations, though outdated, yet still relevant, may be given here.

"The World Health Organization spent about 83 million dollars over 10 years to eradicate smallpox in the world. That amount would not be enough to buy even one of the latest generation super sophisticated bomber aircraft. The cost of WHO's program for the eradication of malaria has been estimated at about 450 million dollars and is proving too high for the world to meet. Yet this amount spread over several years, is only half of what is spent everyday for military purposes and only a third of the reported price of a new Trident nuclear missile submarine."

Again "At the World Food Conference in 1974 it was estimated that development assistance to agriculture needed to be stepped up to five to six billion dollars annually until 1980. Only about half of this target figure is forth coming now. Contribution of funds equivalent to only one percent of the military budget of the industrialized countries would fill the gaps."

On the other side, "Approximately 400,000 scientists and technicians are working all over the world on military projects which consume 40 percent of all funds allocated to research and development from public and private sources."[3]

If we asked, 'Why all these colossal expenditures, and why this preparation?' The reply used to be, 'It is intended to prevent the enemy from attacking us, and even if he attacks, to strike back with double the force.' In other words, the nations, particularly the Nato and Warsaw pact countries were always poised on the brink of war. The late Mr. John Foster Dulles, an early US Secretary of State was said to have expounded and practiced the policy of 'brinkmanship.' It was said that at one time the USA and the USSR had enough arms and nuclear weapons to destroy the whole world, not once, but several times over. Later the Super Powers receded somewhat from the precipice, but armed preparedness continues almost as before. But we can definitely say that the 'Third World War' is a remote possibility. Now the world can breathe a little freely.

But it is hasty to conclude that the world is safe. There may not be a 'Third World War', but local wars have been going on in many parts of the world, thousands are being killed, large scale destruction has been going on, not only of human's dwellings, factories, offices, hospitals etc., but also of irreplaceable, precious natural resources. Think of Kampuchea, Iran, Iraq, Syria, Lebanon, Palestine, Israel, Chechnya, Somalia, Ruanda, Sudan (Darfur), Sri Lanka, former Yugoslavia and so on. Indeed, the danger is not from the big powers, but from the smaller nations of the world. It is they which are spending more on armies and armaments. It is strongly suspected that, apart from India Israel and Pakistan, which have already acquired nuclear capability. North Korea and Iran are on the point of joining the nuclear club.

Now a new, but far more dangerous, menace has been looming over mankind. The terrorism unleashed by the left extremists has been going on in several countries in the East, but it was never on the scale launched by the latest entrant, Islamic fundamentalism. The whole world is terrified of it. It has little concern for life. Its aim is to kill as many people as possible, whether innocent or otherwise, whether they are women, children or aged. That is why its car bombs, suicide bombs (the latter particularly) take place in markets, hospitals, places of worship, festival gatherings or mourners' groups and have plunged the whole world in despair. It is very difficult to trace it. It strikes suddenly and swiftly. That is why even the mighty superpower, the USA, is at a loss how to deal with it. Imagine what would happen if some of these terrorist groups were to acquire nuclear, chemical and deadly biological weapons. Such a possibility cannot be ruled out altogether, considering the latest advances in technology.

We must remember that the majority of mankind is not yet really free. Dictatorships, whether military or otherwise are the rule rather than the exception, it seems. That is why such fiends in human form, Idi Amin of Uganda, Emperor Bokassa of The Central African Republic, Pol Pot of Kampuchea could flourish for sometime touching the lowest depths of depravity and senseless cruelty to which man could sink, Besides in many of the so called democracies too what prevails really is not democracy, but something which militates totally against the basic tenets of democracy, which yet masquerades as one by putting on some external symbols. The elections, the key factor in democracy, are really turned into a farce. It is no wonder corruption and crime have spread their tentacles far and wide into almost every nook and corner of society in almost all the countries. The result is that though the better off sections of society buy peace and security for themselves either through money or power and influence (even they fail now and then in spite of all their advantages), the vast majority of the population, especially in the developing countries of the world, have to reap the bitter fruit of their governments' policies, Even now millions—tens of millions, we should say—steeped in illiteracy and ignorance, now live in inhuman conditions and suffer from malnutrition, disease and hunger. When we say hunger we do not refer only to the great famines such as those that ravaged Ethiopia and Somalia. In almost all the developing countries, especially those of Africa, even though the food is available it does not reach the miserable sections of society.

So in spite of all the wonderful advances we have made, our civilization, and in spite of the great statesmen and leaders of men (or perhaps because of them) we have not been able to free ourselves from wars, bloody conflicts, massacres, genocides, hunger, malnutrition and disease. Is there then no remedy for all these ills? We need not give up hope. We have one sure cure to most of man's ills, if we have the will and strength to use it fully and well. That is intelligence.

It is intelligence that has raised man far above the animals. Physically he cannot compare with many of them. Take for example, an elephant, or a tiger, or even a horse, or a bull. But the biggest, the strongest and the fiercest animals have yielded to man. It is only because of his intelligence. Very early man applied his intelligence to Nature and began to learn her secrets and thus succeeded in gaining more and more mastery over her. He started collecting wealth, developing and consolidating social organization and progressed in civilization. How far man reached in his development at a particular time could be known by the extent of knowledge of Nature he had acquired by then. Especially within the span of the last two centuries man's power over Nature increased by leaps and bounds and he is now almost at the peak of his supremacy. Modern man commands things that could not have been dreamt of even by the mightiest conquerors of the past and he does things that are little short of miracles scarcely possible even for gods in the past. All this is because of the development of science and technology. Science (we can include technology in it, for it is only applied science) is only the systematic and purposive application of human intelligence to gain knowledge of Nature, which includes man himself. So the one basic principle behind all man's achievement and progress is intelligence.

Here a question arises. When all this progress and achievement bear testimony to the fact that man has been using his intelligence, how can we explain the persistence of hunger and disease? Does it not mean that intelligence too has failed? The answer is an emphatic 'no'. It is not the failure of intelligence, but the failure of man to use his intelligence fully and well that is responsible for the present crisis. The three vital fields for the life of man on earth are the political, economic and social fields. Of these again the political field has now become the key one, because it is here that decisions are taken regarding development or delay, order or chaos, peace or war. Because the world has become a closely interrelated one, the decisions taken in the political field affect all other fields and the consequences of such decisions are not confined to the nation concerned, but extend to other countries too and, at times, to the whole world. (This is not to deny the fact that economic and social forces condition political decisions).

It is in the political field (and to an equal extent in the social field and to some extent in the economic field too—in the latter the hard realities compel us to be more practical) we do not allow our intelligence to operate freely and fully. We still cling to crude self-interest, narrow loyalties, irrational notions and prejudices, blind emotions and passions. If we study the causes of recent wars we do not find them much different from what they were, say, some two thousand years ago. Similarly, our politics may have to deal with totally different situations and its scope too may be far wider than it ever was, but the fundamental character of our political decisions and actions has not changed much over the centuries. That is how we can explain the emergence of Hitler in a scientifically and technologically highly advanced nation like Germany (that was, of course, more than half a century ago, but that does not make much difference). Hitlers are still there and the same type of forces he represented such as racism, intolerance, fanaticism, thirst for power, megalomania are still flourishing. Indeed, we are far closer to the savage than we are prepared to admit. Suppose you placed some machine guns or some such highly sophisticated weapons in their hands. You can imagine what would follow. That could be a picture of the twenty first century man holding science and technology in his hands (It is highly exaggerated, of course, but the comparison holds good.) The results are too obvious.

We cannot continue to be unscientific in the age of science without plunging ourselves deeper and deeper into conflict, chaos and self-destruction. Whereas our primitive ancestor with his stone-axes and spears or bows and arrows could at best kill a few men, now a single hydrogen bomb can finish off the lives of a million people. Besides, as has already been remarked, it is utterly inexcusable on our part to knowingly allow millions of our brothers and sisters to die of starvation or disease or to lead their lives in misery and despair. So the situation brooks no delay. We have used intelligence with great success in all other fields. We must extend it to our own personal lives, social, economic and political affairs. Man's intelligence has never failed him and will not fail him in the future. On the physical plane there is no problem that he cannot solve, no difficulty that he cannot face with its help, more particularly with the help of that form of intelligence that is called science.

Here one conjecture—only a conjecture—may be pondered. If immediately after the First World War, in the circumstances prevailing in Germany, the Germans themselves and the victorious powers too had behaved a little more intelligently, probably there would have been no scope for Hitler to rise and capture power and probably there would have been no Second World War and six million Jews and millions of others would not have died unnecessarily. Even if this conjecture is dismissed as of little use, we can yet affirm that intelligence in politics, in private, as well as, social life of man will necessarily bring about a transformation.

We need not go in for unrealistic solutions. We need not call for total giving up of arms. While taking the necessary precautionary measures, we must lay more emphasis on applying our intelligence to our various problems (The justification of armed preparedness here does not mean that the present colossal expenditure is justified. Whatever we are doing now is something absurdly disproportionate to the real needs. It reveals an almost insane preoccupation with desperate remedies. When we start applying intelligence the armament race would naturally slow down.)

But it is easier said than done. Extending intelligence to our politics and personal and social affairs is not easy. It requires a change in our attitudes and ways, involving great pain and discomfort, but it is worth striving for. The gain to humanity thereby will be tremendous. So if we are sincere lovers of humanity, if we want peace on earth and happiness for all, we must determinedly prepare ourselves for the 'Age of Intelligence.'

II: Intelligence in Action

Before we understand what intelligence can do, we must know what it has done so far.[4] So we must start with earliest man. Man is part of the animal world. Purely physically, that is, from the point of view of the structure and function of his body, he has many close similarities with other animals, mainly mammals. If you take the embryos of a man, an ape, a horse, and even those of a lizard and a fish you will be astonished to find how similar they look.

The first men were indeed little distinguishable from the animals. They were just one of the numerous species, with their own peculiarities of shape and movement. And they lived just like animals for long ages. The early man ate the grain that was growing wild like cattle grazing in the field, or ate the fruit that were found on trees like birds or monkeys, or hunted weaker animals like carnivores preying upon deer etc. But slowly, very slowly, over the ages, man began to separate himself from all other animals, even from the apes to which the primitive man bore very close physical resemblance.

Nature is a whimsical goddess. Though she often gives in abundance to her children, at times, she turns them back with a harsh 'no', quite inexplicably and unexpectedly. Their accustomed food becomes unavailable.

At such times the animals are quite helpless, and they simply perish in hundreds and thousands. But man is endowed with intelligence and that makes all the difference. Because of his intelligence he was able, quite early to free himself to some extent from the helpless dependence on Nature.

But we should not be misled by the word, 'intelligence.' What the primitive man had was only a few rudiments of intelligence, the faintest glimmers of it. Even animals show rudiments of intelligence. We can observe this when an animal is in search of food. Hunters, especially big game hunters, have good experience of how an animal understands its surroundings and adapts itself to them, either to evade the hunter, or to attack him. But there is little thought of the future and little learning from the past in the case of animals. When an animal's need—hunger or sex—is satisfied it gives no more thought to it until the need arises again in all its pressing urgency. It cannot plan for the next year's flood or drought. If at all any animal is seen to give up an old course of action and adopt a new one as a result of some past experience—we see many such cases—it is almost always an instinctive action. There is no conscious choice. But with man the case is different. He learns from the past. It is not wholly a case of accumulation of instinctive responses. The primitive man might not have, in the beginning, realized the value of experience all at once.

But when he had the same experience several times he had an inkling of knowledge and he projected that knowledge towards the future. That was where human intelligence began. (The functioning of the brain that relates only the action and the result—direct, we should perhaps add—may be called instinctive and this is what we see in animals. That which relates the past, the present and the future is human intelligence, however feeble or uncertain it might be in the beginning.) Man began to observe Nature by applying his (rudiments of) intelligence and this knowledge gave him some measure of control over her. Instead of merely taking what Nature gave him, he began to take Nature's bounty with his own hands, as it were. He applied his own effort to Nature. His hands were fast becoming perfect instruments of his intelligence. With very rough stones in the beginning and later with polished stone implements he was able to kill animals bigger in size than he. Still later he evolved the bow and the arrow and, sitting or standing in a strategic position, a single man was able to kill a big animal, say a mammoth, the prehistoric ancestor of the elephant, which in earlier times required fifty or even a hundred men to encircle it and kill it with stones. At some point in time he chanced upon the discovery of fire. But at first, he had no idea of its revolutionary significance and vast potentialities. He started using fire to scare animals away, to protect himself from cold, and later to cook his meat. He erected or carved rude shelters to protect himself from the heat of the day and cold of the night and, particularly, from the rain. He began to cover his body, not with cloth yet, but with leaves or bark of trees. An animal must go to a water–source each time to quench its thirst. But primitive man soon (soon may mean in the prehistoric perspective a thousand years, we should remember) learnt to draw and store water. Observing scattered grain sprout, he began to sow them himself and reap the harvest. Thus, he was able to take from Nature more than what was immediately necessary to satisfy his needs. He began to store for the future (at first for a few days and the period increased gradually) and this in course of time liberated him, only to some extent, from being completely at the mercy of Nature. He had time to adopt a different course of action if he met with failure one way. Man was a gregarious animal from the beginning and a rude social grouping began to evolve and family began to stabilize. (Animals and birds have a sort of family life from the mating season till the end of the breeding season, but in each mating season a different partner is likely to be selected.)[5] The first rudiments of language became noticeable. They were no more than cries of anger, grief, pain, surprise, satisfaction or pleasure, but they were far more expressive and better articulated than the cries of animals, and pointed out the object which was the source of pleasure or pain, thus leading to the naming of objects and helping in consolidating the social life of man.

Somewhere about this time the savage time of man came to an end and the civilized stage began. Before we go to the next higher stage, that is, the civilized stage, we must sum up our impressions of primitive savage life.[6] The primitive savage having only a faint glimmer of intelligence, the knowledge he acquired must have been very meager and it must have taken such a long time that he was not fully conscious of having acquired it. His life was full of fears and uncertainties. He saw a demon (the conception of God must have been a later development) or an evil spirit in every shadow, in every stone and tree and even in ordinary natural happenings like the daybreak, coming of night, lightning, thunder, rain, and the advent of spring were all mysterious happenings to him. Even when he was able to make fire he did not feel he had made it. He felt that some mysterious force had helped him. He looked at the fire with awe. Even when he hunted animals and killed them he must have felt it was because of the grace of the animal he killed. So he worshipped the animal he killed. The chief happenings in his own life, birth, maturity and death were mysterious events to him. Yet he was slowly fumbling towards connecting cause with effect and conscious manipulation of things.

We proceed to the next stage, the civilized stage. Man arrived at agriculture and domestication of cattle, horses, sheep, etc. He was spinning and weaving cloth, building better shelters that could definitely be called houses, and forming villages.

He evolved the wheel and discovered the lever principle. He started making and melting metals. All these, the discoveries of the wheel, the lever principle, making and melting of metals etc., were momentous events in the life of man. They were all the results of the growth and application of intelligence and they raised man higher and higher above the animal world and even above the primitive man and led him on the path of civilization. Most important of all, very clearly he hit upon the principle of division of labor. This division of labor not only helped man in producing more in less time and thus leading to the formation of wealth, but also gave a vigorous push to the social organization. Society developed and diversified.

The most important event for man, often overlooked or given only a passing mention by historians, is the development of language. Suppose man had no language, he would have been where he was some twenty thousand years ago. Without language human society and civilization cannot be imagined at all. For it is language through which intelligence expresses itself. It was language that gave a shape to human society, consolidated it, stabilized it and gave it a continuous life. It reflected man's life and growth, achievements, his aspirations, and fears. At first, as we have seen, it was a mere collection of sounds expressing a limited range of human emotions and experiences and gradually it extended to the source of those emotions or pleasure or pain, thus leading to the naming of objects. When man was able to name the objects, he could not but try to say something about them. Thus, he started thinking of the relationships between objects and actions. That means he was already moving from the particular to the general, from the concrete to the abstract. All these appear very simple to us, but to the early man they were very difficult, complicated and momentous steps forward. (We hear of some Australian aboriginal tribes which have names for a hundred varieties of eucalyptus tree, for example, but no general term for the tree itself). When man once started coining terms for the general and abstract concepts there was a sudden transformation in him. Literature appeared on the horizon preceded by pictorial arts perhaps. Just as at a certain stage, a boy becomes a man, so also with the liberation of language from the particular and the concrete, man became the man we understand. Thus, we come to the great civilizations of the past: those of India, China, Egypt, Babylon, Assyria and a little later, those of Greece and Rome etc. By that time, physically man had reached the maximum degree of development (some scientists have pointed out that there has generally been a slight increase in the size and weight of man over the last two centuries. But their observations are confined to a few European countries, and further they do not extend sufficiently back into history, so we cannot come to definite conclusions about their observations. But this much we can say that the model of the human form, both from the point of view of physical stature and strength and from an aesthetic point of view, continues to be the ancient Greek, Roman or Indian one.) Man by 3000 B.C. appeared as far removed from the primitive man as the latter himself was removed from the apes. But the more remarkable thing was the sudden flowering of thought and of the creative arts. It was as if in one jump man encompassed the whole universe. When we bring before our mind the achievements of our ancestors, we are filled with wonder, and sometimes with despair, at their richness and diversity. There were many great thinkers (besides poets and artists) who seemed to rise above time and place and unveiled truths that hold good for all time. The power and reach of their thinking amazes us, and if we keep in view the material circumstances of their time, the originality of their thinking is all the more surprising and naturally it is doubtful whether we can ever produce greater thinkers than they. This phenomenon, the sudden spurt of thought and creativity to the greatest heights, a characteristic of intelligence, we shall discuss later. The point here is the primitive stage of man ended and the civilized stage began. The next stage is the modern one, that is of science and technology (But here, with one difference: We do not say that civilized stage ended and the scientific one began. Science is part of civilization. We can say it is only a higher stage of civilization).

When we speak of the stage of civilization, we should not assume that all mankind was in the same stage and that the gradual growth and development of civilization was a uniform one. Nothing is more contrary to the facts. During this stage many of the early civilizations vanished, some almost without trace, some sank into decay, new ones came into existence at different times and with different characteristics and different rates of growth, and many people still remained in the primitive stage.[7] This continued almost up to the fifteenth and sixteenth centuries.

But we can go by the general trend and sum up our impressions of the civilized, pre-scientific stage. Agriculture became widespread, and there was a great variety of agricultural products; cattle gained prominence followed by horses and sheep. Cities came into existence and architecture flourished as it had never before. The stress was on size as well as on beauty. Varieties of clothes and fashions appeared and spinning and weaving were raised to a fine art. Metals were extensively used, handicrafts flourished producing a rich diversity of beautiful as well as useful articles. Money was invented and travel and trade developed. Classes came into existence bringing conflicts inevitably in their train. The most unfortunate development for mankind was, fighting and killing became a profession. Whereas in the primitive stage, tribe fought tribe, now fighting spread to vast areas and war became a hobby as well as the means of power and wealth for the ruling classes. Conquest, plunder and pillage became the rule of the day. Thus, paradoxically, along with man's civilization, man's barbarity and inhumanity to man too increased, or rather increased at a higher rate. Kingdoms grew into empires and millions suffered and died under the oppressive heel of the imperial rulers and conquerors in order that the latter might enjoy luxury, pomp and power. This is all history, and we need not enter into further details here.

The main point is that despite the glory and splendor of the past civilizations, their achievements were more or less individualistic and did not form a continuous, collective activity and so were almost affairs of chance. That was why when a few brilliant individuals died it was a catastrophic and irreparable loss to those civilizations. They continued to flourish for some more time, but with their soul gone, as it were. Further, the achievements of those great men of the past were mainly confined to the realm of ideas and of the heart. In relationship to the physical world around them, even in the case of very ordinary natural phenomena and things of daily life, their achievement was limited and meager.

This contrast between the brilliant achievements of the past civilizations on one side and their miserable deficiencies on the other is all the more striking. We must understand why it was so.

Let us take an illustration. Suppose you must look after some animals, or grow a crop, or fashion some articles out of metal. You have necessarily to be practical.[8] You must work observing certain conditions and wait patiently for the result. Thus, your freedom is curtailed to an extent. But in the realm of ideas and imagination you can roam at your will and go up to the highest reaches your fancy can take you. So, when the intelligent men of the great ancient civilizations discovered the infinite possibilities of idea and imagination, they were eager to explore those new worlds (poetry, drama, philosophy etc.) and were loath to be confined to the cramping, prosaic world of daily life.

Besides, society had already become stratified, and status came into operation. The people who were concerned with agriculture, spinning, weaving, building, extracting and molding metals and other such crafts and practical tasks were given a very low status in society. It was no wonder that the higher classes who had the leisure to cultivate their minds to the full and develop their powers could not think of occupying themselves with the problems of the lower classes.

Agriculture, spinning, and weaving, use of metals etc., were all, we have already seen, the results of the application of intelligence and consequent acquisition of knowledge. But the knowledge did not come suddenly or quickly. It was gathered slowly and laboriously with occasional flashes of genius and discoveries of chance. It was not anything like the dazzling flowering of intelligence in the realms of idea, fancy and beauty. So peasants, craftsmen, workers and such other classes of people plodded on their traditional path, advancing only inch by inch, as it were. One would like to imagine what would have happened if the creative and intellectual energies of the ancient Greeks or Indians had been diverted to the field of crafts and mechanics. One fact cannot be overlooked here. Necessity is the mother of invention, so goes the proverb. In those distant times the intellectual classes did not feel the necessity of increased material knowledge. Life was simpler, for one thing. Secondly being the part of the leisure classes, they were able to enjoy the pleasures of life without straining themselves too much physically. The millions who sweated and toiled did not count much. Whatever be the causes, the pre-scientific civilized stage still rested on a slender basis in the matter of application of intelligence.[9] This situation continued almost up to the end of the fifteenth century in the countries of Western Europe and almost up to the beginning of the twentieth century in the countries of Asia and Africa.

Now we can proceed to the next stage. Already towards the closing years of the fifteenth century some inventions, such as the mariner's compass and the consequent discoveries of America and a sea route to India, gunpowder, and printing tolled the knell of the old order and heralded the advent of a new age in the life of mankind.

The new age is the age of science. Science was not a new boon granted to mankind by kindly providence. Science marked only a stage in the growth and development of intelligence. It is nothing but systematic application of intelligence to the objective reality around us. It is rooted in experiment and proof. Its aim is to gain control over Nature. 'Knowledge is power ' is its motto. As a matter of fact, the discovery of fire, the wheel and the lever principle in those dim distant times could also be called the results of scientific thinking and activity. But they were sporadic, uncertain and brief-lived glimmers of science and almost accidental in nature. Modern science is distinguished by its conscious, continuous and relentless search for facts and the system behind them. Clear evidences of this new stage in the development of intelligence became noticeable around the sixteenth century. Copernicus, Galileo, Harvey and others were the first genuine scientists. Lord Bacon was the philosopher of this new spirit of enquiry. It was he who gave the motto of science that 'Knowledge is power' But science was still a limited activity confined to a few centers and to a few dedicated and determined individuals. It was only after the publication of Newton's *Principia Mathematica* in 1687 that science could be said to have become a steadily swelling stream that grew into a mighty flood by the beginning of the twentieth century. The invention of the steam–engine gave birth to technology in the modern sense. Today science and technology have been developing so fast in all directions that it is almost difficult to keep track of them. While change in the life of the primitive man was visible only over tens of thousands of years or more, and later in the pre-scientific stage of civilization it was noticeable within centuries, now it is compressed into a few years. Compare the history of man since his appearance on the earth to the end of the nineteenth century with that from the beginning of the twentieth century till now: You will have an idea of the colossal transformation brought about by science and technology in the life of man and in the world. Science and technology have also necessitated changes in our social, political and economic institutions. Capitalism, socialism, and even feudalism earlier were all attempts at adjustment to the changes brought about by this new application of intelligence, that is, science, to man's surroundings.

One or two examples will show how science is vastly different from the previous form of intelligence that was the basis of the pre-scientific age of civilization. The ancients—we need not go thousands of years back, even two or three centuries back—had, despite their great achievements in all other fields, little protection against disastrous floods or continuous drought. Floods devastated cities and villages, submerging vast areas, and sometimes put an end to an entire civilization. When there were drought and famine millions perished. Many migrated to other lands. Only those who had stored enough of food-grains to see them through prolonged difficult times survived. But now the fiercest rivers have been tamed by building dams across them and collecting their waters in huge reservoirs. These waters are used to irrigate not only lands that have been under plough for long but also virgin lands. Even deserts are turned into smiling evergreen lands. Though rains cannot be ordered at will, yet experiments have already been going on to make artificial rains. Most of the pests and plants diseases have been controlled. Chemical fertilizers have increased the yield per hectare of almost all agricultural products several times. Above all, after the development of genetics, modern agricultural scientists have brought about quite a stupendous revolution by evolving high-yielding, disease-resistant and almost miraculous strains of seeds. On account of all these factors and on account of the use of machines and scientific techniques, uncertainty in agriculture has largely been removed and the quantity of food that is grown now could not have been imagined by our ancestors even in the wildest of their dreams. The only unfortunate thing is the simultaneous population explosion has literally swallowed up this tremendous increase in food production and thus has not allowed us to realize the magnitude of the achievement of modern science on the agriculture front. And suppose even now, despite all these advances and developments unprecedented floods come, because of our modern communications we have sufficient advance information to take all the preventive and protective measures. And suppose there is famine or shortage of food in any part of the world, food supplies can be rushed there before death can start claiming its victims. Formerly pestilences such as plague, cholera, typhoid, and smallpox took their toll by the million. Even as late as the fifteenth century, 'black death,' it was said, killed nearly half the population of England at that time. But now these epidemics are no longer heard of in the advanced countries.

All this has been possible because of science. Imagine for a moment what would happen if by some miracle we were made to forget all our scientific knowledge. It would not be any wonder if nine-tenths of the population of the world perished in a short time in such circumstances. But science is no miracle. Its achievements may appear miraculous, but its methods and techniques are the farthest from the miraculous. Science has made such progress because it has made everything within its reach sure and certain.

What the scientific method is that has produced such astounding results we shall soon see, but, for the present, it is enough if we note that modern science has been able to give us systematic knowledge, because with its experimental techniques which involve manipulation and control of things it has been able to isolate the exact cause or causes of each thing. Thus, the systematic and exact knowledge has given us all the mastery over nature. Our ancients were no less endowed with brain capacity as we are.

But they had no way of manipulating and controlling things to force all the necessary facts out of Nature, for reasons already explained.

Thus, to repeat, the one basic principle behind all man's development and achievement is intelligence. The various stages of growth and development in the life and civilization of man nearly correspond to the stages in the growth and development of his intelligence. Thus, the history of man up to now is the history of the achievements of intelligence. And the dark side of history is the only result of man's failure to use his intelligence at that level.

Even now, as we have seen, there are vital fields where we do not allow our intelligence to function freely and fully. The results are quite obvious. Our deficiencies and failures appear all the more striking against the background of the spectacular achievements of science and technology. We have also seen the terrible dangers we face and the urgency with which we must pull ourselves out of the present impasse. So, the only remedy is the extension of intelligence to the remaining fields to dispel the darkness that still enshrouds man's personal life and fills it with suffering and misery. Now we are in the age of science. So, when we say intelligence, it means, in the present context, that highly developed form which goes under the name of science.

We must understand how science actually works, but before that we must understand the nature of our thinking, for it is here we have to start the new revolution.

III: Thinking

Intelligence operates through thinking. But all thinking is not intelligent thinking. You can know this by comparing the thinking of an illiterate and ignorant person with that of a highly educated and cultured person. Even primitive men thought in their own primitive way. Without some kind of thinking man would not have progressed at all and would have stayed where he had been among the animals. So, while accepting the fact that all men think, we must understand that all do not think alike. There are various kinds of thinking. We must know about them and see how they differ from, or fall short of, scientific thinking.

First, there is common sense thinking. Common sense means nothing else than the understanding which a person acquires from his own experience and from the experience of others which he learns through tradition, or through his social contacts. Its value depends on the experiences he has and his own capacity to think. Science too originally took its birth in common sense thinking, but soon separated itself from the latter by its open and critical approach and by its relentless pursuit of fact and system. In other words, science is common sense thinking[10] purified of its faults and failings. Conversely, we can say that common sense thinking is one that has not rid itself of its faults and failings.

Scientific thinking demands a high degree of discipline, single-minded devotion and intensive training in its methods and techniques. Ordinary thinking on the other hand, requires no such conditions. It comes of its own to a person as he goes through life. It relies on memory and tradition. It is not orderly and systematic and tends to think of each thing or experience as a separate entity and offers piecemeal explanation and thus lacks consistency. Because it cannot go beyond the particular, it cannot reach out to the universal principles. For example, we see things fall and we are satisfied with the immediate cause. But the same simple fact led Newton to discover the Law of Gravitation which covers the entire universe. And because ordinary thinking has no special equipment or means to probe into things deep enough to discover the underlying interrelations, it is often carried away by superficial matters or events. For example, when an ignorant man sees two things happening one after the other, he assumes the preceding event or thing is the cause and the succeeding one is the effect. (This is the famous fallacy of post hoc, ergo propter hoc Most of the superstitions arise out of this fallacy). But science does not come to such a conclusion unless it satisfies itself by experimentation and research that there is an inevitable connection between the two facts. Ordinary thinking considers what is striking and overlooks what is negative or less striking (though it may be even more important than the former). It arrives at conclusions without caring to know whether it has sufficient and definite evidence to do so. Sometimes the conclusions may not follow from the evidence at all. One very common fallacy of ordinary thinking is what is called false generalization.

Suppose we meet a Chinese gentleman and have an unhappy experience with him; at once we conclude that all the Chinese are deceitful, dogmatic or some such thing. One single experience, and we are ready to condemn a billion Chinese at a stroke: Many popular assessments of nations and peoples partake the character of such false generalizations. They are often expressions of prejudices. (But this does not mean that all general assessments of peoples and nations are totally wrong.) We may have such assessments in our mind when we deal with various peoples, but we must rely mainly on direct observation, for a particular individual may not come under the general assessment.

We need not proceed with this matter any further here, for any book on logic (be it the most elementary one) will point out the fallacies of ordinary thinking and explain them fully with illustrations. It is enough if we keep in mind that ordinary thinking is limited by many factors, and is liable to error and illusion. But this is not to say that ordinary thinking is all false and wrong. Sometimes it is surprisingly true and useful. As has been pointed out, it all depends on the nature of the experience and the nature of thinking that has gone into the particular matter. But as ordinary thinking has no definite means to distinguish between truth and falsehood precisely, truth and falsehood are likely to exist side by side in it and even get mixed up. Naturally it is not entirely reliable. It may sometimes lead us along the right path, but, more often than not, it may mislead us and land us in danger and difficulty. Mankind blundered towards some progress with the help of ordinary thinking (the achievements of geniuses excepted) and only when science displaced it, the progress was remarkable, continuous, steady, and speedy.

Next, we must consider how men think individually and collectively. Individual thinking can be re-divided into objective thinking and subjective thinking. Man does objective thinking when faced with a problem (in the objective world) or as part of his profession or interest. Objective thinking is an exacting, laborious and sometimes painful process. Left to himself man relapses into subjective thinking which is more pleasant and comfortable to him. In fact, most of his free time is taken up with this kind of thinking. Subjective thinking is not thinking in the proper sense. Man is a bundle of dreams and desires, likes and dislikes, feelings and emotions, prejudices and beliefs, and complexes and fixations. Most of his (subjective) thinking is merely giving expression to these dreams, desires etc., or justifying them to himself or to the world. (The latter is called rationalization and is the most common characteristic of individual thinking). Further, man (unconditioned by training or purpose) often allows his emotions to govern his thinking. Emotions have a place in man's life; they are indeed the lifeblood of his activities and experiences, but emotions should be guided by thinking. When, on the other hand, emotions precede thinking and overshadow it, they become dangerous and often prove harmful.

Even when the individual deals with the world around him and moves in it, he starts with the capital 'I', that is, he looks at the world from his own point of view (which is conditioned, as we have seen, by his dreams, desires, likes, dislikes, past experiences etc.) He loves his family and friends, he loves his community and country and, at times, he thinks of the wider humanity too with goodwill. But it is 'my family', 'my friends', 'my class or community', 'my town or region', 'my country and so on all the time, (Of course, he says our country when he is among his compatriots. He does so similarly in the case of region, class or community etc.) The pull is always towards the center. That is why when he thinks of humanity he thinks of his nation first, when he thinks of his country he places his party, class, community or region above it and when he thinks of his community, he places his family above it and at the peak stands the 'I'. It is a descending order of loyalties from self to the world. This ego-centric point of view does not, however necessarily mean selfishness. A father thinks solely of his son's welfare and is ready to sacrifice for his sake, but the son's welfare is as he conceives it to be. It is no wonder that often the son turns against his loving parent and earns the epithet 'ungrateful wretch'. He has his own point of view after all! Thus, a man may not be selfish, yet he cannot escape his own self.

Thus, as each looks at the world from his own point of view, the individual rarely admits an objective standard. He is his own standard. That is why when there is disagreement between two persons there is no effort to probe into the real causes of their disagreement, that is, to refer to facts. Each thinks of the other as unreasonable, prejudiced, narrow-minded and so on. That is how discussions among ordinary people generate more heat than light and spread ill will and rancor rather than understanding and cooperation.

There is also little consistency in the individual thinking except, of course, the consistent influence of the 'I'. The individual is dominated by the particular, the present, and the striking. His memory is the only record to check himself. But this memory often plays tricks and is equally under the pressure of the moment. It is a common experience that when someone points out that, on a previous occasion, he said something quite different to what he is saying now, the latter often reacts with the words, 'I did not say so.' If the former is persistent and comes out with concrete proof, the latter is discomfited and tries to explain away his inconsistency and, at the same time, he is angry with the other for showing up his fault.

All this does not however mean that every individual is, without exception, irrational, emotional and narrow-minded. There are many wise and clear-thinking persons who can save not only themselves but others too from error and difficulty. Even ordinary people listen to reason in their calmer moments, that is, when things do not touch them too deeply. The purpose in the foregoing description is only to point out the errors and limitations of individual thinking generally.

But one fundamental fact seems to have been overlooked in the discussion above. There is no individual apart from society. Society has not been considered at all. It is an undeniable fact that an individual is far more a social product than he imagines. He is born into society (which pre-exists him and survives him too), he grows in it, lives in it and is thus constantly under its all-pervasive influence. His experiences, thoughts and feelings are all conditioned by it. The very language he uses is a social product and is the means by which the individual is bound to society inseparably. His mind too, in the final analysis, turns out to be a social product to a very large extent.

But let us not go to the other extreme and claim that man is totally a social product. If each individual is entirely a social product there should be complete uniformity among all the individuals forming society. But we find wide and remarkable differences among the individuals not only of a nation but also of a community and even of a family. The reason is this: Man is not a mere clod of clay. He is a sensitive organism and thus acts and reacts in his own turn upon society (just as he acts and reacts upon Nature). Besides, society is an indeterminate entity. We must distinguish between its various constituents. As the child grows, he is first under the immediate influence of his mother and, or, nurse, later under that of his family and friends. As he grows up, he comes into the wider circles of society like school, college, community, religion, class, nation and so on and is subjected to their influence. The closer and earlier the factors, the greater and deeper their influence.[11] Thus, in the end, how an individual is molded and formed depends to a great extent on what sort of experiences, feelings, and thoughts he has, what sort of family, school, and community he has grown up in and lives in.

Special mention should be made of the influence of economic factors on human thinking—individual as well as collective. The economic system, the productive relations, the job we work at, the materials and tools we use, our working milieu have all their influence on us directly or indirectly in various ways. Even great philosophers, poets, writers, and others, it is said, cannot completely escape the influence of economic factors.

But let us once again remind ourselves that all these factors only condition an individual and they do not determine him entirely. How an individual acts and reacts is the final deciding factor. A highly rational individual can re-mold his personality and free himself from cramping, narrow influences, prejudices and errors. That is how we can explain the emergence of great men who seem to be above time and place. But even a genius cannot completely cut himself off from society. Society and its particular constituents continue to influence him to some extent. Even when one rebels, the very way one rebels is often conditioned by the experiences one has in society. Thus, it is true that individuals cannot exist apart from society, but it is equally true that each individual is unique in his own way.

But just as individuals cannot exist apart from society, society too cannot exist apart from the individuals constituting it. It is not an organism that lives by itself. It exists only in the individuals, or rather we should say, in the minds of the individuals. So, what sort of society it is, depends on what sort of individuals constitute it. Naturally what we have noted about individual thinking applies equally to social (or collective) thinking. But social thinking is not a mere aggregate of the thinking of all the individuals. Men act and react upon one another, both individually and collectively. When people come together some of the individual failings and errors may be corrected and more accurate and comprehensive ideas and views may emerge. But it also happens that individual errors, prejudices etc., gain greater currency when they enter into social thinking and become powerful and all-pervasive. We know the force of tribalism, racism, parochialism, narrow nationalism etc. We sometimes see that a person who in his private life is mild and reasonable becomes fanatical and violent when he becomes part of a mob. Anyhow society consists of all sorts of individuals: some may be great thinkers, some creative artists, some emotional-minded people, some ignorant beings, some introverts and some extroverts and the thinking of all these people enters into social thinking. That is why social thinking is a strange amalgam of wisdom and ignorance, reason and superstition, prejudice and fair-mindedness.[12]

We have thus seen the characteristics of various kinds of non-scientific thinking and their inherent weaknesses and limitations, and the errors they are prone to.

Only scientific thinking has freed itself of all these weaknesses and faults and achieved universal validity. It is because it is not concerned with the thinker himself (unless he is himself the object of study) but with the objective facts. It does not matter whether one is white, black or brown; Hindu, Muslim or Christian; weak or strong; rich or poor. So long as one thinks objectively and adopts the necessary techniques and methods to find out the facts and the system behind them, one will contribute to the expansion of definite and systematic knowledge of Nature. (The extent and value of one's contribution, of course, depends on one's personal capacity and, secondly, on the availability of the relevant facts).

It is the non-scientific kinds of thinking with all their limitations and errors that have so far prevailed in the vital fields of man, namely, the political, social and economic fields. The results of such a situation are all too clear. So it is imperative that we extend science to the above-mentioned three fields and also to our personal lives.

IV: Scientific Thinking

The idea of extending science to political, social and economic fields and to personal affairs may lead some people to imagine a situation where human beings would be treated as laboratory animals, to be experimented upon, so that scientific laws could be discovered and applied accurately and effectively. They may even have in their minds, visions of a science-dominated world as described in scientific fantasies—a world where babies would be produced in huge laboratories by the fertilization of separately preserved ova by stored spermatozoa in artificial wombs, and where later the same babies would be reared and educated on strictly scientific lines, where there would be no more need for family ties and other such relationships, where people would sustain themselves on nutrition tablets, where in fact, man would be reduced to the condition of a robot. It is indeed a nightmarish prospect and shows what scientific visionaries might do with the world if only they had their own way. But we are not concerned with such visions. We are concerned only with the living present and the immediate future.

The reason for the fear as described above is that when one thinks of science, one generally thinks of the physical sciences only. But physics and chemistry are not the whole of science. They are just two of its innumerable branches. The practical methods and techniques of each science (which naturally means, each branch of science) differ from those of others. The methods of physics and biology are not the same. Nor are the methods of biology and psychology. Why, even the methods of physics and chemistry differ. The nature of the particular field of study determines the type of practical methods and techniques to be employed. What is common to all sciences is the scientific approach or attitude. And the scientific approach is only the systematic and purposeful use of intelligence in order to gain knowledge of nature, which includes man himself.

We can understand this better if we know how scientists work in general. But first of all, let us take note of two fundamental principles of science. They are that (1) The universe of fact is a harmonious whole. All the facts of the universe are consistent with one another. Facts are never contradictory. (2) the universe of fact is cosmos, not chaos. There is order, certainty, regularity, system in the interrelation of all facts of the universe.[13] That these are not mere assumptions is proved by the history of science.

A scientist, as long as he is a scientist, is engaged in observing and collecting facts (mostly by performing experiments), classifying and analyzing them. The universe of fact being cosmos, the scientist is sure to find interconnections among the facts under study. On the basis of his findings he formulates a hypothesis to explain those facts into a system[14] and verifies his hypothesis by devising and conducting fresh experiments (that is, referring back to facts again). After thorough and repeated verification he propounds a theory, and this theory can be called one more extension of man's knowledge of Nature, small or big depending on its scope and application.

The description given above of the way scientists work is oversimplified and is bound to draw serious protests from the scientists themselves. For one thing, facts do not lie, as it were, on the roadside, waiting to be picked up by any passing scientist. They have often to be forced out of unwilling Nature. For this purpose, the scientist causes changes and disturbances in Nature and even breaks things up and conducts rigorous experiments in order to collect facts thoroughly and precisely. That is why modern science has developed highly sophisticated apparatus and machines and equally highly sophisticated experimental techniques. And that is how science has come to be divided into various highly specialized branches, each requiring years of study and practical experience. Secondly, the scientist is not concerned with all the facts of the world. Facts are numberless and endless. Mere observation and collection of facts as they come do not lead the scientist anywhere. He is concerned only with the relevant facts, that is, those facts that have bearing on his subject of study. The words 'relevant facts' naturally suggest that the scientist starts with an idea in his mind as to which facts he must look for. This means that he has a sort of working hypothesis even before he starts collecting facts—that is, quite the reverse of what I have stated above.

But this does not, however, mean that the scientist starts with some pre-conceived notion and selects only those facts that are to his liking or that suit his pet theory and suppresses or overlooks others that are inconvenient or contradictory. It would be wholly misreading the nature and function of science. The initial idea or working hypothesis is only to assist the scientist in achieving his objective: knowing systematically about the object of his study. If he has no such initial idea or working hypothesis, he may be working and working without achieving anything. (A trained detective discovers many facts that escape the ordinary observer, because he knows what sort of facts to look for and how to look for them). The scientist does not cling to his pet theory in the face of facts. The verification of his own hypothesis tells him whether he is in the right direction or not. When the facts tell him otherwise, he is ready to modify his hypothesis accordingly, and is even prepared to discard it and adopt a new one in the light of his findings. Thus, we cannot say which comes first: the hypothesis or the facts (just as we cannot answer the question: which came first, the egg or the chicken). Sometimes a hypothesis—a wonderful stroke of imagination on the part of a genius—leads to the discovery of strange and breathtaking facts and sometimes a chance fact starts a scientist thinking on entirely new lines. At whatever point one may start, the circle must be completed; facts—hypothesis (or theory)—facts. But it is an ever-widening circle comprehending more and more knowledge.

Further, as soon as the scientist has come to a definite conclusion regarding his hypothesis which can now be called a theory,[15] he publishes it so that other scientists spread over the world and working in the same field or in allied fields may take note of it, verify it for themselves by carrying out their own experiments. There is thus nothing secretive about science (if governments do not interfere in the name of security). The original scientist gives all the necessary data and states clearly the conditions under which the theory applies.

Even when a theory is established it is always subject to scrutiny and testing and is liable to be changed or discarded when new facts come to light that seem to contradict it. That is why the laws of science (which mean nothing more than thoroughly verified generalizations having wide application) are not laws in the political or legal sense. They are only statements of certain uniformities in the group or groups of facts concerned and serve us as guides in dealing with the group or groups of facts.

When an apparently contradictory fact is discovered, it is not suppressed; on the other hand, it is studied with greater care to see whether it may not lead to similar facts and thus reveal a new view of things. The contradiction must be explained—not explained away—by fitting it into a wider system that resolves the apparent contradiction. For example, when we pull the two ends of a string with our hands, our right hand seems to be working against the left, but both are working for the same purpose: to snap the string into two. Thus, the universe of fact being a harmonious whole, the various theories of science can never be contradictory to one another. Not only the various theories of a particular branch of science, but also those of all the branches can never be contradictory to one another. The discoveries of physics and chemistry, for example, cannot be contradictory to those of biology. Of course, the interrelationships of all the theories, of all the branches of science, that is, of the universal system, may not be found all at once, but the principles given at the beginning of this chapter form the foundation of science without which it cannot exist, much less grow, at all. Thus, science is not mere knowledge, but systematic knowledge and this has to be always kept in mind.

This in turn leads us to the most prominent characteristic of science. Science respects no authority save the authority of fact The words 'sacred' and 'holy' are not to be found in the dictionary of science. Prejudices, likes and dislikes, feelings, and emotions cannot and should not interfere with it. Thus, science means a relentless pursuit of systematic knowledge and a scientist never allows anything to come in his way of acquiring or extending that knowledge.

Finally, we should never lose sight of the fact that science is a cumulative social activity. Science has made such tremendous strides and encompassed the whole universe, because hundreds and thousands of scientists have worked and have been working selflessly for the extension of knowledge. The modern laboratories, apparatuses and machines bear testimony to the collective effort. A theory is often the result of several scientists working together along with their assistants and other workers, though often under the supervision and guidance of one or two eminent scientists. (All the scientists need not be at the same place. If their work is coordinated, they can be said to be working together). A genius may, by a flash of his creative imagination take science miles ahead in a single stride. We have the cases of Galileo, Newton, Darwin, Max Planck, Einstein and Niels Bohr, but even such a genius does not start from nothing. Each generation stands on the shoulders of the previous one. So, the genius too starts from where his predecessors left. And he owes something to his contemporaries too. Besides, his very language, his very mind are social products after all (of course with certain qualifications as we have seen in the previous chapter).

All this brings before our mind once again the nature and functioning of modern science into bold relief. The word modern should be kept in mind, for we often hear of ancient Greek sciences, ancient Indian science and so on, and we have also seen that the discovery of fire, the extraction and use of metals, the development of agriculture etc., were all basically scientific in nature. But modern science distinguishes itself by its continuous, collective, cumulative and systematic social activity rooted in experiment and proof. There is still scope for chance (that is, chance discoveries) but it has been reduced to the minimum. Similarly, geniuses still have their unique place and value, but modern science is no longer entirely dependent on them. Suppose Darwin had not been born, even then the Theory of Evolution would have been discovered sooner or later. Similar is the case with the work of other great scientists too. The steady and relentless advance of science would have uncovered the relevant facts in the course of time, and those facts would have revealed their inter-connections and thus led to the system behind them. The history of science, particularly in the twentieth century, bears ample testimony to this trend. We hear of several scientists working independently arriving at the same type of findings or discoveries. This is not to deny the role of geniuses, but only to stress the main characteristics of modern science. Individually we may not compare with some of the great thinkers of the past, but the knowledge we have gathered through science places us far above all the previous generations of men. That is why whereas in the case of ancient civilizations, it was a sudden flowering of thought and activity followed by stagnation and decay, in the case of modern science it is an ever-continuing and ever-spreading process.

All this should not lead us to imagine that scientists are a sort of supermen. Scientists too are human beings after all, with their own faults and failings. Outside their particular fields some of them may be as irrational and credulous as any layman.[16] To such scientists scientific method is only a tool to be used in a certain way to achieve certain results. Scientific outlook may not condition the whole of their thinking. But that in their respective fields and in so far as they have stuck to the scientific method, they have done extremely well is proved by the results. Secondly, it is not that there are no disagreements and disputes among scientists. There are, and they are often fierce and endless. But these disagreements relate generally to interpretations and not to facts. A black cat cannot be black to some and white to others. But when sufficient scope is not there for experimentation and precise study, there are bound to be different conclusions and different interpretations. But these differences and disputes are not personal, emotional or national. Nothing is hidden partly or wholly, nothing is distorted. That is why the scientists try to resolve their differences by searching more rigorously for all the relevant facts. Thus these disagreements and disputes really act as spurs to urge science ever forward. They do not allow it to relapse into conformity and purposelessness. On the whole, however, the mighty achievements of science clearly show that agreement is far more prevalent among scientists than disagreements.

Now after this long description of the way scientists work in general (even this description is oversimplified, it has to be admitted) we can conclude that the scientific approach is only the continuous, critical and purposive exercise of intelligence to gain systematic knowledge of Nature (which includes man himself) mainly with a practical goal in mind.

The Value of The Scientific Approach

The scientific approach that is embodied in the method described above has, wherever it is applied, yielded a world of knowledge to man. Such knowledge is not for mere adornment. As Francis Bacon has said, 'Knowledge is power'.[17] That is how man has almost become the master of the world. Science has changed the world beyond recognition. Yet, we should remember once again that modern science is hardly four centuries old. Compare its achievements with those in other fields. In art, literature, philosophy, ethics, and religion, we cannot boast of greater achievements than those of our ancestors centuries ago, or even thousands of years ago. The revolution we see around us is almost wholly the revolution of science.

Thus, we have applied the scientific approach with superb success to the earth, the planets and the stars, to the animate and the inanimate (remember the Theory of Evolution and the revolution it has brought about in our understanding of life and its development), to the human body (remember the amazing discoveries of medicine and surgery) and even to the human mind (remember the discoveries of psychology and psychoanalysis) and to other fields. Then why should we not extend the same approach to those vital fields of man where it has not been applied fully and continuously so far? Is it wrong to know thoroughly and systematically about our political, social, and economic matters, and our own personal affairs and act in the light of that knowledge? Should we believe in the adage that 'Ignorance is bliss?

But can man ever live and act in utter ignorance? Can you do a thing without knowing what it is and how to do it? Can you go to a place without knowing what sort of conveyances are available and where? Can you operate a machine without knowing how it works? Can you deal successfully with people whom you do not know or understand? Can you distinguish the genuine from the false, the friend from the foe?

Of course, animals carry on their lives without knowledge. They live by what is called instinct (which, in other words, means inborn behavior pattern.) But when their 'instinct' fails—as when some change in the environment that does not suit their instinct overtakes them—they simply perish. Man would never like to fall back to the level of an animal, and even if he wanted to, he would not succeed fully. Man has given up his instinct in the pursuit of freedom of action to such an extent that he cannot recover it fully.

One example already cited will show the value and indispensability of systematic knowledge to man. We have seen what devastation epidemics such as plague and cholera caused till a few centuries ago. There was no sure protection against these epidemics, because man had no definite knowledge how they originated and how they spread. Millions died helplessly. The epidemics were thought of as visitations of God to punish the people for their sins. (But sinners alone did not die; even innocent persons perished in great numbers!) But later, science gave man the knowledge about those epidemics and because of that knowledge he was able to conquer them, so much so that in most of the countries (except in the very backward ones) they are almost unknown today.

As long as we are ignorant, we are at the mercy of every change in Nature. We are each confined to a little, cramped, dark world peopled by innumerable fears and dangers. As our knowledge increases, so too does the range and scope of our activities and, on the other side, the fears and dangers recede proportionately. Referring back to one example given above, when we do not know anything about the people with whom we have to deal, we are quite helpless. Necessity drives us to observe and understand and as our understanding of the people increases so too does our confidence and ability in dealing with them. Thus, we can say we enjoy freedom in proportion to our knowledge. And this knowledge gives us power of control over our surroundings. All the discoveries and inventions of science prove this. So to repeat: Knowledge is freedom and Knowledge is power.

Coming to the vital fields already mentioned: suppose we are faced with a difficult and dangerous situation. Can we deal with it better when we know what causes and circumstances have created the particular situation or when we do not know anything about them, but proceed on some assumptions for which we have no proof? Similarly, in our own personal affairs, suppose we failed in a certain matter: then would it not be better if we did some cool and critical analysis of the failure. The causes might be purely external or they might lie within us. Would it not be foolish to blame others or other things when the fault lay within us, or to blame ourselves unnecessarily when the causes lay elsewhere? When we know the causes we may not succeed at once, but we can, at least, try to take the necessary steps in the light of that knowledge. We are not concerned here with the goodness or badness, or justifiability or otherwise of the causes. A long nurtured grievance, a narrow loyalty, a prejudice, or some blind emotion or sentiment may be at the root of the matter. Whatever it may be, it is better to know it than not to know it. Our actions can be surer and more positive then.

But when we say causes we mean 'real' causes and not apparent ones. Politicians and social leaders and other such people are adept at offering 'good' causes. But we should not be misled by their claims. It is here science is of the greatest help to us. It is not guided by outward appearances, but probes into the real causes and brings out all the facts before us. What we do with those facts depends on us, yet it is beyond doubt that systematic and accurate knowledge is better than half knowledge or ignorance.

An analogy may be apt here. Suppose the waters of a river are polluted and there is a consequent hazard to the health and life of the people of a city situated on its banks. It is also known that a factory is located on its bank and that it has been letting off its effluents into the river waters. Should the people of the city simply assume that the factory alone is responsible for the pollution and demand its shutting down and removal. (Let us say that the factory produces something worthwhile for the community and also provides employment to a sizable section of the population of the city, and, further, the location is justified from the economic point of view—cheap river transport, requirement of large quantities of water and easy means of disposing of the wastes etc.). In the usual course of things there will be a clamor and an agitation for the removal of the factory, splits and divisions among the people, some agitating for the removal, others opposed to it, mutual accusations and recriminations and consequently clashes and even violence may follow. But if we proceed scientifically and get the water examined we may come to know that the factory is not really responsible for the pollution. Even if it is responsible, it may not be the only cause. Further, even if the factory is found to be the sole cause of the pollution; by scientific research and experimentation, methods may be discovered to dispose of the wastes without resulting in harmful pollution, and then the factory can be retained (with all the consequent advantages) and yet the pollution checked. The example given above is far too simple, political, social, economic, and personal issues are far more complicated, one may say. Hence, the greater is the need for scientific knowledge.

Here one question arises: when the advantages of science are so obvious why would anybody resist it? But it is not so simple as that. Let us take an example here. Suppose a friend of yours has a very ugly habit. You are sincerely interested in his welfare and so point it out to him and advise him to give it up for his own benefit. But does he take your criticism in all sweet reasonableness? No, the chances are ten to one that he will take offence and bear a grudge against you for your criticism, well-meant though it may be. It is because he has come to consider his ugly habit too as a part of himself and so the criticism as an attack upon himself. It has already been pointed out that man is a bundle of dreams, desires, likes and dislikes, feelings and emotions, prejudices and beliefs and complexes and fixations. All these become part and parcel of his personality. So long as any change concerns only outward objects, a person does not resist it much, and sometimes even welcomes it, but when a change involves the giving up any of the things that he has come to consider as part of his personality it is excruciatingly painful to him like a major operation without anesthesia. He resists it. Science in the vital fields of man poses such a change.

Secondly, there are vested interests to which change poses a challenge to their authority and a danger to their very existence too. Science has often destroyed many a grand and solemn-looking edifice housing the vested interests. Naturally science was the most unwelcome thing in the beginning, and earlier scientists had to face ruthless suppression and persecution. For example, there was the 'new' knowledge that the planets including the earth went round the sun and not otherwise as it had been believed so far. What harm could such knowledge have done to the ordinary life of the people? But look at the facts. The great book of Copernicus, which first propounded the theory, was not published until after his death for fear of the storm the revolutionary findings would raise. Giardono Bruno was burnt at the stakes for his urging of free enquiry. Galileo was imprisoned and forced to recant because he had discovered the satellites of Jupiter through his newly invented telescope and proved the superiority of the Copernican theory. The Church feared that these discoveries and enquires would undermine its authority and its very existence would be at stake and so reacted in the way as described above.

It was only in the nineteenth century that science could be said to have gained respect and recognition, and even then it was expected to keep off from man. But science could not be bound and restrained in that way. When Darwin published his Theory of Evolution and revealed the truth about the origin of man there was a sort of earthquake in the Western world. People as well as the vested interests reacted violently to his theory. When Marx propounded his theory of capitalism there was another great shock. When Freud in the early part of the twentieth century probed deep into the human psyche and came out with observations that upset the long-established notions of purity and innocence they evoked feelings of disgust and revulsion.

So too science in private lives, in society, in the political and economic fields would be unsettling in the beginning and put the people to some discomfort and force them to painful readjustment. Naturally they would not welcome it willingly. But it is worth the trouble and discomfort, for the gain would be tremendous in the end. But there are vested interests in society, in the political and economic fields too, just as once the Church was the vested interest that tried to block the way of science. Whatever be the vested interests, they must be fought, and people have to be shaken out of their lethargy and indifference and be made to open their minds to the light and breeze of a new dawn.

To sum up we should not rush to hasty conclusions or generalizations. Nor should we blindly apply generalizations—theories or impressions. We should stick to facts. How we should proceed with facts has already been described. We need not proceed on strictly scientific lines, but should avoid faults and fallacies. In effect we have to think about our own thinking and make it an efficient means to achieve truth, beauty and goodness in our lives.

V: The Necessary Corollary of Thinking: Planning

It has been pointed out that the motto of modern science is : 'Knowledge is power'. It is because its main purpose is practical, science has made the tremendous progress we see all around. When we acquire knowledge of anything we at once think of using it. When we seek systematic knowledge of our politics, society, and economics, and of our own private lives, we do so in order to apply it for our own benefit. The application of knowledge gained in these most vital fields inevitably leads to planning.

There was a time when the very word 'planning' was a sort of red rag to many. (The same attitude seems to be gaining strength once again). Planning was felt to lead to regimentation of life and suppression of individual freedom. One eminent economist once even argued that it was planning that led to fascism in Italy, Nazism in Germany and communism (or rather, Stalinism) in Russia, and so we should do away with all planning. It was a wonderful argument, but only the gentleman looked at the matter standing on his head. Really it was not planning that led to fascism, Nazism, and communism. It was the other way round. Fascism, Nazism and communism came first and after seizing power they made use of planning to achieve their objectives, just as they made use of so many other achievements of science.

We often see that burglars, bank robbers, swindlers and even murderers (cold blooded murderers, of course, and not those who kill in a fit of passion) plan their crimes beforehand—the more the experience and knowledge (knowledge of the scene, the situation, the persons involved etc.,) the more thorough and systematic their planning will be and the consequent success in execution.

Here we see one use of planning. So, should we say that planning is criminal because it leads to burglary, bank robbery, swindling and murder? It would be like saying that driving a fast car is bad because a criminal drove in a fast car to the scene of the crime and fled again in it. It is not planning that makes the criminal. The criminal is already there. He makes use of planning (we should rather say, he plans, for planning is not an objective entity, but only a way of acting) because it is the only way to achieve his objective and avoid detection later. (Of course, he is often caught, not because of his planning, but because he has overlooked some detail or details, or because of some unexpected turn of events for which he has not planned). A half-baked criminal plans very poorly and is caught redhanded. The detectives of crime themselves must plan equally thoroughly to trace the criminal.

But planning is not necessarily related to crime. It is found in all fields of life. Planning means nothing else than intelligent anticipation and the necessary preparation. It is making use of our knowledge to achieve our objectives. Can a businessman, though he may be the bitterest opponent of governmental planning, do without a plan in his own firm or factory? Can we build a house, undertake a long journey, choose a career, celebrate a function (say, a marriage), conduct a conference, or do anything worthwhile without a plan? Perhaps we can blunder through somehow without planning, but the result will often be ridiculous and, at times, disastrous too.

But think of a government that concerns millions of people (or, for that matter, any large organization). Can it do without planning at all? Can it put into effect some sweeping reform, a huge program or project or carry on a war without planning at all? The budget of a country itself is a piece of planning. An individual can, at times, as has been pointed out above, do without planning, for the consequences are confined to himself. But organizations and governments cannot do without planning on the condition that they do something worthwhile.

Yet why does some unconscious antipathy to planning persist in the minds of many people? It is only because of some confusion in their own minds. An analogy may be helpful here. There are the rules and regulations. To some they appear as curbs on freedom. But suppose there were no traffic rules and regulations. Then what would happen? We cannot but admit that these rules and regulations actually protect and extend our freedom. So may the rules and regulations in other fields too. (This is not to defend every rule or regulation. What determines the value of a particular rule or regulation is what lies behind it. We shall come to this aspect presently). Next imagine a game like hockey, football, or cricket without any rules whatsoever. Then all the joy of the game would vanish. The game would cease to be a game at all. It would be boring to the spectators, as well as to the players. Imagine an orchestra with each member banging away at his instrument without a program (planning) and coordination (represented by the conductor).

This takes us to the main point. There is no inherent contradiction between planning and freedom. The real contradiction is only between freedom and ignorance. An ignorant man is not only a slave of circumstance, but also a slave of his own brutish nature. As man gains knowledge, so too he gains control over himself, as well as over his surroundings. The one lesson we learn from the history of science and civilization is that man's freedom has been directly proportionate to the increase in his knowledge.

Planning implies knowledge. If there is no knowledge, there can be no planning too. If the knowledge is thorough and systematic, the planning will also be perfect and successful. If the knowledge is partial and faulty the planning also will be imperfect and faulty. So, if there is anything wrong with the planning we can understand there is something wrong with the knowledge behind it. That is how when we feel certain rules and regulations are irksome and restrictive, we can see that they represent not reason and understanding, but arrogant authority and prejudiced or faulty thinking. The same can be said of laws. Laws that embody intelligence will advance freedom and contribute to progress, but laws that embody mere authority shackle man and obstruct his progress. We can indeed say that man's progress can be measured by the degree of approximation of statutory laws to scientific laws.

Man always wants to know and when he knows he cannot but plan (for planning, to repeat, is only intelligent doing or acting). So to condemn planning is to condemn knowledge and ask man to give up his intelligence and live by instinct and chance. Nobody would surely like to go back to the state of animals which live without planning.

Secondly, we should remember that planning is intended to realize certain objectives. The objectives can be good as well as bad (as we have seen in the case of criminals). Whatever be the objectives, we cannot but plan if we want to realize them. So the goodness or badness of objectives should not be confused with goodness or badness of planning. There is nothing good or bad about planning at all. It is either perfect or imperfect, successful or unsuccessful. The goodness or badness relates only to the objectives.

Even in visualizing or fixing objectives, knowledge has a part. You can know this by studying the character of the objectives of an intelligent and cultured person and of an ignorant and uncultured one. The objectives of the latter are vague, unrealistic and often contradictory, if he has any at all. Those of the former show the depth of his experience and breadth of his vision. They are definite, realistic and harmonious with one another.

If we take all these facts into consideration we find that planning is not only desirable but also inevitable for intelligent beings. That is why perhaps, the word 'planning' has ceased to rouse as much hostility as it used to do once. Indeed, planning has become a prestigious word for modern politicians.

But when planning is sought to be extended to a whole country which amounts to full planning—the usual word is 'total planning' but I would rather use the word 'full planning', for 'total planning'[18] smacks of totalitarianism—there is a lurking fear in the minds of many that full planning may lead to suppression of individual freedom and regimentation of life. They have the example of communist countries before them. When planning is only an intelligent way of acting how can planning itself, even if it be for the whole society, lead to suppression of individual freedom? The causes for the latter must be located elsewhere and not in planning itself. The Soviet Union or any other communist country was not the model of planning. There was planning certainly, but it was not the planning as advocated here.

The suppression of individual freedom and the strict regimentation lay not in planning but in the dogma that ruled those countries. In spite of its scientific claims it was a closed ideology that could not tolerate deviation or dissent. This dogma governed the objectives of planning in those countries. Secondly, if planning there involved great hardship to the people it was because of imperfect or faulty knowledge.

We have seen that social sciences have to follow a somewhat different course from the other sciences and that they have necessarily to adopt the subjective line of inquiry too. We have also seen that each individual is unique in his own way. So, when we think of society, we must take into account the interplay of individual aspirations, longings and needs. That is, we can have full scientific knowledge of man and society only if all the individuals freely participate in it. Thus, democracy in the real sense is an absolute prerequisite for the full functioning of science. To the extent democracy is not there knowledge too suffers proportionately. This lack of democracy and the governing dogma made the communist society a closed and unfree one and vitiated planning to that extent. So, it was dictatorship and dogma that affected planning and not the other way round.

To repeat, it was not planning that led to communism. Communism (as a doctrine) was there before planning started. If despite the dogma, and in spite of the suppression of individual freedom, the Soviet Union and other communist countries made such progress, it was only because of planning.[19]

So planning is a necessary corollary of science, whether it be in politics, economics, or any other social science If our knowledge is full, free and systematic and our objectives noble and we have the determination to achieve them, planning will make us realize our goals, while extending our freedom at the same time. To sum up, freedom is only where there is intelligence. And intelligence operates only in a planned way. Planning is totally different from regimentation, for planning is based on intelligence (it may be imperfect and muddled, that is a different matter) while regimentation is based mainly on authority.

VI: Limitations of Scientific Thinking

The readers may, by now, come to feel that the high sounding appeal for the application of intelligence to man's private and public affairs turns out in the end to be nothing more than an appeal for a further extension of the scientific approach. Science being the most systematized and practical form of intelligence, application of intelligence to man's problems will necessarily mean the extension of the scientific approach to them. But it is not exactly that. In this chapter we shall discuss some of the serious limitations of science and how science cannot mean everything for man. Man's life comprehends many more things than science can ever reach. It is intelligence far wider than science, that covers the other aspects of man. It is not mere science but intelligence in the true sense that reveals the fundamental unity of all human knowledge and experience. That is why the main theme of this book is that we should work for the age of intelligence. We are already in the age of science. That is not enough, we must move still far ahead.

Failings of Individual Scientists

Before we think of the limitations of science we have first to beware of some of the failings of individual scientists. As science has advanced it has led to extreme specialization too. The more limited the area and the more the concentration, the more thorough and definite our knowledge will be: that is the principle behind this scientific specialization. In fact, human experience proceeds through fragmentation. We eat morsel by morsel. We see motion only in a series of stationary pictures piling upon one another. Time and space also must be broken up into sizeable units in order to understand and experience them. This does not however mean that man is condemned to have only disconnected and fragmentary knowledge. Man can see the whole behind the parts, the system behind the individual facts. Even though what we actually see are the stationary pictures we have the idea and experience of motion. Similarly with time and space and other things. But in this age of extreme specialization there is the danger of the specialist studying the leaf forgetting the tree. Science, we have seen, is not mere knowledge but systematic knowledge. To forget the connecting links with the wider system is to cut the branch which one stands on. Not only the work of the scientist who completely forgets the wider system is distorted, but also the knowledge he provides us will be misleading and dangerous. So along with specialization continuous effort must be made to coordinate the findings of various scientists and fit them into a system.

There is another failing of individual scientists closely akin to the above. When a scientist has discovered something that has far-reaching or revolutionary implications, he is naturally carried away by over-enthusiasm. We have the classic example of Marx and Freud. Marx discovered a very important principle behind the development of society: the influence of productive relations on social and political institutions and that was a momentous discovery. His discovery has changed our very conception of history, and it has revolutionized our understanding of man and society. Similarly, Freud discovered a vast dark world underneath the conscious mind. This too was a momentous discovery. Since then, Freud's theories have conditioned our thinking regarding man's mind and actions. In an earlier age Marx and Freud would have been burnt at the stake for their discoveries. They were fortunate in that they lived in an age when science was generally accepted. Yet the implications of their discoveries were such that they had to face a great deal of disbelief, prejudice and bitter opposition. So they had to assert themselves and fight prejudice and disbelief and overcome opposition and gain acceptance. Naturally they had to take a fighting and aggressive stand.

This, in course of time, led them to an extreme position from which they overlooked all other factors and looked at the world from their own point of view.[20] it does not mean that Marx and Freud alone took up such positions. There were others too—some of the behaviorists, geneticists and others do even now. (That is why this general observation.) But their points of view did not have as much revolutionary significance or impact as those of Marx and Freud had. We have seen that he is no scientist who accepts only those facts that are to his liking and overlooks others. So, we can say that extreme positions often become unscientific positions. Such theorists not only over-emphasize their own point of view to the exclusion of others, but also begin to look at all things from that particular angle only. Their point of view becomes a prejudice which is against the spirit of science. Those who set themselves up as scientific messiahs and try to create a following are not scientific at all. And those who describe themselves as belonging to a particular school of thought such as Marxism, psychoanalysis have simply misunderstood the spirit of science. We can compare all such theorists and followers to the six blind men who tried to describe the elephant. One of the blind men caught hold of the tail and said that the elephant was like a broom-stick. He was correct in so far as he was describing the part he caught hold of. His error was only in forgetting that it was only a part he was dealing with and the elephant was much more than that part.

It is here we must note an important caution. Suppose there is a biologist. If he says something about astronomy we do not give his views the same respect as we do to his views on biology, unless we are sure that he has as much knowledge of astronomy as he has of biology and so has the necessary authority to speak about astronomy too. So when we hear pronouncements from scientists we have to see how much authority they have in making them. Further some scientists are tempted to venture into philosophy. There is nothing wrong in that, for they are thus only trying to find out the connections with the still larger system. But we should not confuse such philosophical speculations with their scientific work. We should treat each kind with the regard they deserve.

In this connection a common failing of some philosophers, especially those that claim to have based themselves on science, must be pointed out. There is a tendency on their part to erect a philosophy on some striking discoveries and inventions of science. Philosophy should be based on the general principles of science but not on any particular application of it—unless it be of fundamental nature. We know how the principle of the 'survival of the fittest' of the Theory of Evolution was brought in to justify fascism. Science marches relentlessly forward—not in one single direction, but in a thousand directions at the same time. There may also be sudden changes of direction and crisscrossing of roads. So it may abandon many doctrines and theories as out of date and useless. Naturally philosophies erected on such doctrines and theories may fall by the wayside. This applies even to materialism by and large. But this is not to decry philosophizing on science totally. Philosophical implications of new developments can be sought, but raising a whole philosophical structure on the basis of particular findings is not wise.

While being alert to note where a scientist has ventured outside the field of his authority, we must beware of another weakness of some of the scientists. Science is not a mere collection of facts, but a system of facts. So long as facts are not explained, that is, their interrelationships are not brought out, they do not strictly enter the domain of science. But there happen to be some facts and experiences which cannot be explained and which cannot be observed or measured in the usual objective way. While scientists may or may not express their views on such facts or experiences (such views are only individual and extra-scientific) they should never go to the length of denying the very existence of such facts and experiences. It is overstepping the limits of science. Scientists should stick to the facts which are within their purview and which they can explain. But some overlook this caution and make assertions for which they do not have the authority of science.

A word must be said about a recent tendency among scientists, especially among political scientists and other social scientists. It is the excessive pre-occupation with concepts and terminological niceties. There is no doubt that highly complex subjects require very careful definitions of concepts and elaborate and precise terminology. But the danger is it can be carried to extremes. The craftsman who is carried away by the great delight of refining and decorating his tools is likely to forget that they (the tools) are mainly for use. So too extreme preoccupation with definition of concepts and terminological problems may make one forget the very things for which they are intended.

Secondly, it may create an illusion of discovery and progress where there is none. Whatever may be the justification for such preoccupation in other sciences, there is none in the social sciences, more especially in political science. These sciences are concerned with people and people are the most important part of social and political processes. So to keep social or political knowledge out of the reach of the people by making an unnecessary mystery of things which are in fact simple is inexcusable. At least the knowledge should be comprehensible to the average educated person. One corrective to this tendency seems to be to ask the scientists themselves (all scientists, especially political and social scientists) to explain their own theories and findings to the people. Thereby scientists are never likely to lose their moorings. There is another failing of some scientists. When faced with some inconvenient facts which are not amenable for explanation, they try to dismiss them or minimize their significance or try to explain them away. That is wrong. A true scientist should be honest and admit his inability. He should never try to treat facts as non-facts simply because they cannot be explained

Limitations Of Science

Now we must consider the limitations of science. Science and scientific method are not all. This warning is very necessary, for here and there we come across persons who make a religion of science and want to establish its sole empire in the minds of men. Science should never become a religion and it should never be above man.

There is a real fear among many sensitive people that since scientific inquiry is like a scorching ray, the beautiful arts, the sweet dreams, the heartwarming sentiments and emotions, and the soul-satisfying thoughts and experiences may all die and disappear. Life may become one vast blazing desert. This is the very doubt that was raised in the beginning of the fourth chapter, that if science were the sole sovereign of the world, life might become mechanical and man might be reduced to the condition of a robot.

It should be clearly stated that under no circumstances should science become our master, but should only be our loyal servant. It places knowledge in our hands. What we do with it is left to us in the end. The goal of science is man and not otherwise.

Suppose somebody has made an elaborate research and come out with the finding that people over the age of seventy are generally useless: they simply eat away our limited resources, contributing little in return. In former times when the Red Indians of one tribe had to migrate to new hunting grounds, they left their old and helpless people behind, with a stock of food to last just for a few days so that the latter would die gradually of starvation or be killed and eaten up by the wolves.[21] In Africa one tribe, it was said, had a way of getting rid of their old and useless people. They would push the old one up a tree and then shake it vigorously. If the old one fell and landed on his or her head or back and died, that would be a good riddance. If the old one was a little tough and survived somehow, he or she would be allowed to live for another period, and set to washing pots and pans in the meanwhile. Should we too do this with our old parents and grandparents because scientific knowledge has told us that they are relatively useless? We are after all human beings with sentiments and affections. We have a memory of the past and a consequent gratitude to the old for what they did for us when we ourselves were weak and helpless. So in spite of our knowledge, we may choose not only to keep alive our old people, but also to see to their comforts to the last.

Similarly, someone may come out with the statement of what saving it would make and what benefits it would bring if we surrendered our sovereignty to some big power and became a constituent state within it. The statistics might be all right, but we do not choose to act upon them, for we have certain other reasons that are far more compelling to us than mere monetary or other such considerations.

Some science enthusiasts do not understand this, and they overstep their bounds and proclaim that sentiments and emotions have no place in science, simply because they (sentiments and emotions) do not agree with their calculations and are often not amenable to scientific treatment. Formerly writers on political economy used to center their discussions on a supposed economic man—how the economic man would behave in particular circumstances and so on. Later the practice was given up as an entirely absurd one. Such fragmentation of man leads us away from reality. The whole is not the mere sum of the parts, we find.

Man to be understood has to be taken as a whole. Man is not a simple material or organism, but a highly complex being ruled by desires, feelings, ideas, beliefs, sentiments etc. Science, if it is true science, must take the whole man, that is, man with all his desires, feelings, beliefs and sentiments. For the purpose in hand, it may concern itself with a particular aspect, but it should never forget, more so deny, the value and importance of other aspects of man.

Science can, and should, give us knowledge of our needs and resources and help us in visualizing and realizing our objectives, but it cannot decide the objectives for us. Other factors of man's personality play a great part in determining the objectives. These factors cannot be wholly explained in physical terms.

There is no rational ground why one should continue to love one's mother even after one grows up. In animals we see that once the young ones outgrow their dependence on their parents, there is no further relationship of parents and offspring. They are only animals, male or female, weak or strong, that is all. In their case motherhood is a state of the body of a certain duration in certain circumstances. But with us it is a sentiment that lasts lifelong. We cherish the bonds of family. Similarly, we cherish our loyalty to our friends, group, community, nation and even to the whole of humanity (at times, of course!). We love even the animal world and plant world and try to preserve every species from extinction. An old house may strictly be useless for purpose of habitation, but it may still have unlimited value in our eyes, and we would rather sacrifice anything than let it be destroyed. The statues of Abu Simbel could have been allowed to be submerged by the rising waters of the Nile near the Aswan High Dam rather than spend so many millions of dollars on rescuing them and re-erecting them on a fresh site. But the whole enlightened world rose to save those statues just as it would rush to the help of a nation that had been ravaged by some natural calamity.

There could be no sufficient explanation why a small nation, Vietnam, should put up such a long, bitter, unyielding fight against the mightiest power on earth, or how a most and persistently, persecuted nation was able to build a homeland (Israel) against the most adverse circumstances. Why should men sacrifice their lives for the sake of others, or for the sake of a nation or a cause? There can be no scientific explanation why men should set out to scale the uninhabitable, ice-covered peaks of the Himalayas and risk death and disaster. Why should a prince renounce all the pleasures of royalty and seek suffering and penance and preach the eight-fold path?[22] why should a king renounce the use of arms in the very hour of victory?[23] Why should a shepherd boy become a shepherd of souls through the centuries?[24] Why should a middle-aged camel-driver suddenly become a prophet of a new and powerful faith?[25] Why should a weak, timid boy develop into the mighty leader of six hundred million (at that time)?[26] However carefully we study the background of these great men, we shall not find the real cause, because a million others might have had the same background and yet not have had the spark. Can we assert, or at least hope, that we can produce a better dramatist and poet than Kalidasa or Shakespeare? We need not go up to Kalidasa or Shakespeare? Take any other great poet of any country. We can see that he is unique in his own way and cannot be reproduced. This is explained by the dictum; 'poets are born and not made'. The same is the case with great painters, artists, music composers and such other geniuses. We can perhaps by prolonged and intensive research explain some of the things that went into their makeup, the forces that molded them, their deficiencies and faults, and to some extent, their achievement too, but the main secret of their uniqueness will ever elude us. If it were otherwise we would have by now turned out hundreds of Kalidasas, Shakespeares, Tyagarajas,[27] Beethovens, Turners and others.[28] As one scientist once wrote pessimistically, we may develop in many ways and reach hitherto unimagined heights, yet may not excel the ancient Greek thinkers and writers or the Upanishad sages of India in their particular fields.

And there are so many other things beyond the reach of science. The sentiments of love and affection, love of beauty, laughter, the joy of arts and literature, the intuition of man, the power of the will, the spirit of adventure and sacrifice, the hunger for things spiritual, the need for a meaning in life—all these and many more may never be explained in purely scientific terms. All these things may not strictly be necessary for life on earth. The sentiment of love and affection etc., may be of our own making. The beauties we see, the joys we derive are in our own minds perhaps. But without these things life would not be worth living for most of us.

What role has science in our appreciation of, say, Kalidasa or Shakespeare's plays; Shelly or Tagore's poetry; the frescoes of Ajanta or the paintings of Raphael, Rembrandt, Rubens, Titians, Turner, Van Gogh, or Velasquez or the music compositions of Beethoven or Tyagaraja?

It is enough if we realize that science has its limits and that other things too are important for man.

VII: Beyond Science

In the nineteenth century when the physical achievements of science dazzled the eyes of the people and made them imagine the unlimited possibilities of the use of science, it came to be believed that in the course of time science would explain everything and thus give us control over everything, and then nothing would be left to faith and religion; religion would simply vanish. It was also believed that religion was something totally contradictory to the spirit of science and that a scientist should necessarily be an atheist. Materialism and determinism ruled the day. Of course, as a reaction there was also the idealist view of life. And religious people of authority felt science to be their enemy and tried to resist the invasion with their Holy Books and bare hands. But now after the development of cosmology and nuclear sciences on the one side, and of biology and psychology on the other and after the discovery of the Theory of Relativity, the Quantum Theory and the Uncertainty Principle, materialism and idealism (not the zeal for an ideal, but only a school of philosophy is meant here) have lost much of their relevance and use too. Now scientists in general have grown wiser and think it prudent not to pronounce on things they cannot definitely prove or disprove. They carry on their research calmly and quietly. (But there are exceptions, as has already been pointed out).

Let us start with 'life.' There are several hypotheses how it may have come about, but there is no way to prove them. And now in view of the latest developments in Astronomy which raise the possibility of life in other planets in other star systems and galaxies, may be millions of light years distant, and of life totally different from that on our planet, the full explanation of "life', even if ever remotely possible, is eons away.

However, let us have a look around life on our planet in all its abundance and diversity. Let us observe the following facts (only a very small sample, really) and question and ponder over them.

Let us start with bacteria, the simplest and smallest organisms. (They come under plant life actually.). They can exist, it is said, even in high temperatures and even in strong acid baths. How have they got this ability? We know of the battle against the diseases caused by bacteria and the development of more and more powerful antibiotics. The surprising thing is along with the development of antibiotics there is increasing resistance on the part of bacteria on the other hand. Let us say we have discovered a certain antibiotic which acts unfailingly against a certain kind of disease-causing bacteria. Well, the bacteria that which face the antibiotic die. But how can the bacteria which have not faced the same fate develop the mechanism to resist the particular antibiotic?

The same is the case with 'Virus' which is something between the living and the non-living. Outside the living body it is just like any material. But once it enters the body it acts like any living organism—let us say, like bacteria. There is the virus causing Hepatitis B (which is said to be more dangerous than HIV.) We have developed vaccines and medicines to fight it, but now we discover that there is a new strain called Hepatitis C which is resistant to the vaccines and medicines so far developed. How can the virus outside the body, which is like a non-living substance, develop a new resistant strain?

Before we leave the world of bacteria we must take note of one peculiar example, it is a protozoa (single–celled organism) called "Clavellina", described by Julian Huxley in his Essays on Popular Science. Normally it has a particular form with a stomach, a heart, a pharynx, an inhalant siphon and ganglion. But in adverse circumstances it gives up all these organs and reduces itself to a minute ball, five or six times less than its original size, covers itself with a protective film and becomes a cyst and in that condition can remain any number of years. When times are good again it becomes a full-sized organism with all its organs as usual. How has the simple single–celled organism acquired or developed this mechanism? Julian Huxley wonders whether "death" as is generally understood has any meaning with reference to it. One more example: A certain jellyfish-like thing called Turritopsis nutricula, 5mm in size. It has eight to eighty tentacles. Eggs are formed in its stomach. They are called polyps. All these become jellyfish in two days. While other jellyfish die after sometime, this turns back into a polyp again and produces several more polyps. The cycle starts again. Thus, there seems to be no death for this being too. How can we explain it?

Let us turn to "camouflage" an adoptive technique seen in some insects, moths, frogs, snakes and many other living beings, which is very essential for their survival. Take the Tiger. Apart from its lithe body and beautiful yet terror–striking form epitomizing strength, power and ferocity, see how its yellow skin with its blackish-brown stripes provides it perfect camouflage in the dense, tropical jungles. But did any individual of the species study the environment, devise the pattern and pass it on to the offspring? It is simply impossible; it is in the very species itself. But could we say that the species planned that form and design and implemented it? The answer is a "No."

Some scientists tried to explain the phenomenon by the play of light and chemicals. Take the stick insect. When it stands on a dried-up branch you cannot distinguish it. So perfect is its exact resemblance to the dried twigs and leaves. There is another insect which resembles not a dried leaf but a live green one. How can you explain its exact resemblance with the serrated form, the veins, the sub–veins etc.? Here the resemblance is with the parts of a totally different species (plants and trees.) How can we explain it? In this connection one peculiar example must be brought to the notice of the readers. The plant bug (Membracide) mimics exactly, not merely an ant, but an ant carrying a small leaf. How is it possible? Indeed, the world of camouflage reveals not really hundreds, but thousands of varieties. Observe them and study them carefully and think deeply and see if you can convince yourself it is a mere play of light and chemicals (in the atmosphere or surroundings. Only a pictorial presentation of this subject will have the necessary impact on our minds. But I cannot give the pictures here.)

Let us turn to the migration of birds. Migratory birds make long flights every year and they have no maps or navigation tools. Yet they find their way unerringly to far away destinations. We shall take only one or two examples. The Siberian cranes travel more than 4,000 miles to reach their destination (various spots) in India. Not only that, when the spot they used to visit was found inhospitable they would go to a different one and come to the spot exactly next year. They do not move in an uncertain or helter-skelter way. They all go together in a symmetrical manner and in an assured way. The lead position is changed among them. There is aerodynamics involved in their flight. Do they consult each other and move in that fashion? Do they teach their offspring all this knowledge? Some scientists say navigation skills are in their genes themselves. How have those skills found themselves in the genes?

Take the beautiful Monarch butterflies. Each September the butterflies begin a 5,470 km journey from the forests of eastern Canada and parts of the U.S. to mountains in the Michoacan State in Mexico. They return north in late march. The thing is the life of a Monarch butterfly is only one month. So the butterflies that migrate and return are not the original ones, but those of five generations later. How do these later generations know the original routes taken by their predecessors some generations earlier to and fro between Canada and the U.S. and Mexico? (In this connection the case of salmon fish is also worth studying.)

Take the bees. How they recognize the right flowers, the source of the nectar, the raw product of honey, how they communicate that information to the other bees (they have certain dance styles, it is said), how they convert the nectar into honey, how they build their hives and they look after the offspring are all explained by entomologists and apiarists, but the question is how have bees acquired the knowledge and techniques?

One thing more. The bees are social insects. They have various categories. One queen has to be in each hive (until new ones develop) whose duty is only to lay eggs. There are drones whose business is to mate with the queen and there are worker bees which gather nectar, prepare honey, build the hive and look after the eggs and pupae (before they develop into full-blooded bees.) The surprising thing is the drone when once it mates dies. Its body structure is built in such a way. Similarly if any bee loses its sting in protecting the hive it dies. All these have individual lives, yet their life is planned as part of the life of the whole society of bees outside their bodies. How can we explain the phenomenon? In fact, a study of bees in all aspects will be very interesting as well as enlightening.

Another thing we notice in nature is the mutual dependence of the species. A vast number of plants depend on bees, butterflies and such other insects for cross pollination and thus secure the survival of the species. Bees, we have already seen, depend on flowers to get the nectar which they turn into food (honey.) Without bees and butterflies etc., many of our gardens and crops would be lost. The horticulturists know too well the importance of bees and butterflies. (According to one estimate the value of food that is produced based on bees is $250 billion.) What we have to note is that the flowers are built in such a way that while providing nectar they see that the legs and other limbs of the bees and butterflies are dusted with pollen. The bees and butterflies too are built in such a way that they serve the purpose of the flowers very well. How has the interdependence of flowers and bees and butterflies, belonging to different species (that too totally different branches—plants and animals), come about?

Take the carnivores and their pray. The carnivores depend on the deer, hares and other such herbivorous creatures. Is it nature's plan that the latter should feed the carnivores? Is that why the latter species reproduce in such plentiful numbers, that, while providing the beasts and birds of prey their food and facing other risks and disasters of life yet their species survive? Just twenty four hares are said to produce in their life time thirty million offspring. On the other hand the beasts of prey such as lions, tigers etc., produce in limited numbers. (Tigers some times are known to eat their own cubs.) This interdependence and balance in nature we can understand and explain, but how it has come about we do not know.

Another surprising aspect of this interdependence may be noted. We are proud of our human bodies, but we may overlook the fact that within our bodies there are millions of microbes. These microbes in our bodies take part in our digestive process. If we completely clean our bodies of these organisms our very life may be at risk. Are our bodies planned in such a way that they need outside organisms too for their full function?

Another example of balance or coordination: if you take our reproductive system, we see that though the female and male bodies are differently planned, their sexual organs are completely complementary and perfectly coordinated to serve their basic purpose. Who planned it? Take our body: The various sensory organs: the heart, the lungs, the other internal organs are all so complex yet coordinated. Thousands of books have had to be written by specialists to describe or explain their function and purpose. If we study the function of each small part of our body we are filled with surprise and wonder.

Not only coordination and balance but also there is beauty too—in form, pattern and design. I need not give examples. They are all around us. Take any specimen of the hundreds of thousands of species: each reveals some special characteristics, some special ways of the propagation of the species, seeking nourishment, protecting itself and living its life fully. All these innumerable facts (they are not non-facts, if we are honest, we must admit them) lead us to a general idea of life (though we cannot answer the question: 'why? In fact, we should start with the plants and trees, how they propagate their species, how they seek nourishment, how they protect themselves etc., and question ourselves how it is all possible.)

We have also to take note of deep-sea life. Where we do not expect much life, we find a rich profusion. It is estimated that about 38,000 species exist in the dark depths of the oceans. We must note that at thousands of feet depth the pressure is intense. It is said to be a ton per every square inch. And it is total darkness. How can any living things exist there? If ordinary surface sea creatures go there they simply die. Suppose we do not know swimming. And we have no aids too. If we plunge into the ocean what happens? Our divers, deep sea investigators always have special equipment. So there is no question of those deep sea creatures going there and adapting themselves to those conditions. Only if they are born with the necessary physical structures they can survive there.

In this context one interesting example must be cited. Take the Portuguese-man-of-war. It is not a single animal, but a well-organized colony of modified, related creatures. One animal forms a gas-filled float, several others join to form stinging tentacles for fishing, a third is responsible for reproduction, while a fourth digests the food which is shared by the whole colony. This beautiful but deadly creature is called technically Physalis. These separate, though related, animals might have come together at one time. But how do they join the same way for generations together and further perform diverse functions to live together in a colony almost like a single animal?

This leads us to certain characteristics of life. It is that life is itself creative. As pointed out just now, it is not a question of species adapting themselves to the conditions and acquiring the necessary structures and techniques. That adaptation occurs within the organism, in the very genes. We may say that life comes up ready with answers to possible questions; solutions to possible problems. Sometimes the answers may not fit the questions well or fully, then life retracts and comes up with (slightly or greatly) different answers. It is always the life coming up with ideas, not otherwise. If we take dinosaurs and other such monstrous creatures of the Jurassic age we can call their enormous profusion and sudden extinction the evolution's mistake. Some scientists tried to explain their demise as a result of the landing of a huge meteorite on the earth. Even if that accident had not happened those species would have come to an end sooner or later. The answer (of evolution) proved wrong. A giraffe's neck is very long, bestowing certain advantages on the species. But the disadvantages are too many. So that line of species is very limited. We are now worried over the extinction of several species because of man, but even before the arrival of man several species went out of existence—the mammoth, the mastodon, the saber-toothed tiger etc., but on the whole life's answers for most of the time are more correct than wrong. Thus there is no pre-determined design in evolution. The design evolved along with evolution of life from the uni-cellular to the multi-cellular, from the invertebrates to vertebrates, from sea to land and so on. Not only is it ready with 'answers', but also always it explores new avenues and possibilities and tries to be ready with newer answers. Indeed, in the words of the famous French philosopher, Henri Bergson, it should be called 'creative evolution.'[29]

Another noteworthy fact is the resilience of life. Not only does it try to come up in the most inhospitable regions, but also its capacity to resurrect itself is often evident. A huge fire may destroy thousands of hectares of forest, but after sometime little greens appear here and there in the burnt out remains and soon the greenery spreads and soon other life too—insects, birds and animals—make their appearance. Similarly, after an earthquake, a mighty flood, or the eruption of a volcano it is life that always wins the battle. The Theory of Evolution brought the idea of the 'survival of the fittest', which has been put to misuse by evil-minded persons. But if we observe the progress of evolution, we notice that as life progresses from simple to complex, the earlier simple ones have all not disappeared. They still exist. Even the most delicate, the weakest continue to eke out their existence. (The primitive fish Coelanthus is only one example.).

All this fills us with mystery and wonder. When we say mystery we do not belittle the role of science. It is science that has revealed the vast panorama of life. It is science that has discovered and classified the thousands of species and their ways of life. But the mystery is there. It is science again that has revealed so much and the mystery behind it. All the facts mentioned above are not non-facts, as already pointed out. They are only a tiny sample of the world of fact around us. As we look at it, think about it, meditate upon it we are surely filled with wonder and mystery. There are those who dismiss all these facts as of no consequence, turn their heads away from it all and then say, 'Where is mystery? There is no such thing. It is only a figment of the mind, a self-delusion.' Of these we can only say in the vein of the poet (was it Wordsworth? it should be) who said, 'The yellow daffodil by the riverside is a mere daffodil to him'

In this connection it is worth quoting American lawyer and politician, William Jennings Bryan. He said; "I have observed the power of watermelon seed. It has the power of drawing from the ground and through itself 200,000 times its weight. When you can tell me how it takes this material and out of it colors an outside surface beyond the imitation of art, and forms inside of it a white rind and within that again a red heart, thickly inlaid with black seeds, each of which in turn capable of drawing through itself 200,000 times its weight—when you can explain to me the mystery of a watermelon, you can ask me to explain the mystery of God."

Let us turn our heads upwards and look at the skies.

Let us start with the origin of the universe. What was it like before the so-called 'big bang' occurred? It is called a singularity. What does it mean? It means it was a state which had no form, no mass, no color, no characteristics, nothing at all we can describe in words. But does that singularity mean an earlier universe, or a series of universes which existed for sometime and then collapsed into that state like stars collapsing into black holes? We cannot know. Well, let us leave the indescribable. Let us come to the 'big bang.' Why did it occur? Rationalists always speak of cause and effect. Can they explain or at least make a reasonable guess what could have caused the singularity to explode in a 'big bang'? Surely something must have caused that 'event.' Well, let us leave the cause of the 'big bang' too. The very word suggests that a sort of explosion must have happened. But then how much time it must have taken? Astronomers say that it occurred in one third trillionth of a trillionth of a trillionth of a second. We may perhaps imagine half a second or even quarter of a second, but trillionths of a second—how can we understand? A new development, nano technology has come about and scientists speak of nanoseconds, nanometers etc., But what is a nanosecond before a trillionths of a second? There was the singularity and there was the universe, that was all.

What is the size of the universe? There can never be a correct estimate, but a scientific estimate (different from a guess because it has some—not all—facts to base its estimate on) is that there are like a billion galaxies. The farthest detectable galaxies are about 7×10^9 light years away and are receding with a speed 2/5ths that of a light year. (Light travels at the rate of 186,000 miles per second. The distance that it covers in a year is called a light year. This unit of measurement is used in dealing with the distances in the universe, which otherwise would require unwieldy and confusing long rows of zeroes.) The Milky Way (not the center of the universe, as we do not know whether there is a center or not) to which our solar system belongs, is one such galaxy. It is said to contain roughly 10^{11} (a trillion) stars. If you start counting them, one per second it will take 3,600 years to complete the counting. (Then what about the billion galaxies?) It is about 105 light years across and rotates around its own axis (if it can be called so) at the rate of 206 miles per second and it takes 200 to 300 million years to complete one revolution. Our sun is after all one (not necessarily the biggest) of the trillion stars of our galaxy. What is the size of the sun? We can imagine it from the fact that one million earths can fit into the sun. Is all this not sufficient to imagine the vastness of the universe? Really it exceeds our imagination a million times, but at least we can have a vague idea of the infinity.

It is generally agreed that our universe is an expanding one. (We have already noted the fact above) But why is it expanding? Normally the Law of Gravity should apply. It is the force of gravity that keeps our earth and the other planets going around the sun in their orbits, otherwise they would have flown away into the space. Then why does not this force apply in the case of the galaxies? It is said that dark energy is responsible for this. But what is this 'dark energy?' The very name suggests that we can never know about it.

Now scientists are thinking of the presence of life not only in our own galaxy but also in other bodies in other galaxies. Even if ever one such presence is detected we can never know about it fully. One writer humorously remarked that if there were beings on a planet some 2,000 odd light years distant to us and if they analyzed the light coming from the earth, they would still see Jesus Christ delivering his sermons (for it is light that gives us sight.) Recently scientists recorded the death of a star 240 light years away. What we have been doing so far is only observing the light that must have traveled millions of light years to reach us. Yes, we are only observers and shall be so for ever. Suppose we ourselves want to send a message to such a planet or star: let us say there is a planet 10 million light years distant, which suggests the possibility of the existence of life: Our message takes 10 million light years to reach that planet. If there is a response it again takes another 10 million light years. Where will we be then? Does this not show we can never know fully. We may perhaps know only a tiny fraction of the world of fact around us.

Let us turn from macro to micro. Until the early years of the last century the atom was believed to be indivisible. That laid the great basis for materialism. But now even a child knows that the atom is not final. We know not only of electrons, protons and neutrons, but also of subatomic particles. Einstein's formula $E=MC^2$ has smashed the primacy of matter. Now the Uncertainty Principle reveals that a particle can never be known per se. As one scientist (M. Stephenson) in *Animal Camouflage* (an early Pelican book) remarked, 'Matter is after all only transitional electronic energy.'

Thus, when we look around us, at our own living world, or at the universe above us, or into the micro world of the atom we are filled with a feeling of mystery and wonder that makes us at the same time humble before the vast reality. Out of these feelings faith arises. Religion takes its birth here. Faith is only belief. Belief requires no proof and can offer no proof. Faith fulfils a basic need of man. As when we walk alone in an unknown area in utter darkness we whistle loudly in order to keep away the fear of loneliness, so also we need this faith to give us courage and confidence as we are faced with the mysterious universe. When faith takes concrete shape it becomes a religion. What religion offers cannot stand scientific scrutiny, but it is comforting and assuring to our hearts and gives a purpose and direction to life. Why should anybody object to it? Religion has been there since real man arrived. And it too has evolved like any other activity of man. Is there no difference between primitive faiths, early religions with human sacrifices and the modern ones? Why, do we not see a vast difference between the God of the Old Testament and the God of Jesus's conception in the New Testament? Some people do not object to religion as a personal matter, but they object to the organized religion. The latter, they feel, is authoritarian and full of corruption and vice. But we must note that people having the same inclination to religion tend to come together. And organized religion with its elaborate rituals, festivities and activities fills man's life with a rich diversity, which otherwise would be like a dreary desert. Organized religion has several ills, of course. But which institution of man is free of any dark spot? It is not an intelligent way to concentrate one's attention only on some dark spots and condemn the whole thing. We must view a thing from all sides, take all aspects into consideration and decide what to do with the ills associated with it.

It is true that organized religion in the past often identified itself with the authorities and the prevailing social and political system, whether feudalism, absolute monarchy, capitalism and even fascism and threw its lot with exploiters, imperialists and even with cruel tyrants and served to keep the masses in subjection and misery. Institutionalized religion was itself often an exploiter, owning vast properties and growing fat and corrupt at the expense of suffering masses. It also perpetrated unimaginable inhumanities (like burning at the stake all those it suspected of heresy and those who were inconvenient to it.) It was the cause of murder, war and loot all carried under holy approval. Not only that, there are cases of those in authority indulging in debauchery and other vices under the cloak of religion. Yes, all this is true, but is that all? For example, if we take only the T.N.T., the atom bombs, the hydrogen bombs, the ICBMs, poison gas and other such devices of death and destruction and the ills of industrialization into consideration what is the picture of science we get? But does it tell us all about science?

And then think of those who actively tried to root out religion and what they have done? It turned out that Stalin and Mao, who did not believe in God and suppressed religion with a heavy hand, were responsible for the greatest number of deaths of men in recent times and they claimed that they worked for the uplift of the oppressed classes of mankind.[30]

There is another aspect of religion which is as bright and noble as the other is horrifying. Many a popular movement and many an urgent reform owed its inspiration to the message and teachings of religion. (Think of the messages of Buddha, Jesus Christ and Mohammed and the times they were heard) If religion aligned itself with the prevailing social and political system, it had also its part in overthrowing many an old system and ushering in a new order. Religion was used by monarchs to humble the mighty feudal lords, and Protestantism lent its support to the emerging capitalism as against feudalism. Many who advocated democracy and even socialism were influenced by religion. It can flourish under socialism just as it had under feudalism and as it does under capitalism. If religion committed barbarities and inhumanities, it also put an end to many an evil and ghastly practice. It made savages into civilized men. Many a noble soul worked for the good of mankind and they believed strongly in religion.

Further religion itself was the only refuge for knowledge and learning when everywhere else there was the darkness of ignorance and it did a great deal to keep the light of knowledge burning, as can be seen from the fact that most of the early universities in India, Britain, France and other countries were religious ones. Not only that, Roger Bacon (not

Sir Francis Bacon who was considered the first philosopher of science), the first one to conduct scientific experiments was a Franciscan friar. Mendel, the father of modern genetics, belonged to a monastery. Many others who could be called early scientists belonged to some religious order or other. Even now many of the scientists profess their faith in God and religion.

To come to the most important and most valuable part of man's life: literature, the arts (painting, sculpture etc.) music, dance, drama and architecture—in all these religions played the most significant part and even now in all these fields its (religion's) role continues to be strong. If we want to banish religion and anything associated with it, it would be no exaggeration to say that more than four-fifths of world's literature, the arts, music and architecture would be lost to mankind. We can never fill the void that would be created if all these which drew inspiration from religion were forced out of existence. For example, you cannot sing of death and sorrow as you can of love and marriage. Similarly, you cannot sing of modern civilized life as you can of religious emotion and experience. Do you not feel differently when you stand in a modern building and when you stand in a church, or a temple, or a mosque?

In this connection we must have a look at the kind of literature, the arts, music and architecture that flourished in Stalin's Russia and Mao's China. Then we can understand the significance of the inspiration of religion.

All this does not mean that everybody should belong to some religion or other. It is only that one should understand that religion is an integral part of life for many and that it has been there for ages and will continue to be in the future too.

It also does not mean that we should overlook its darker aspects. As intelligent people we should observe and study the good and the bad of such things and take the necessary steps to counter any antisocial and harmful consequences arising out of them.

Let us go through some of them. Religion is based on belief. Everybody knows and admits it. For belief there can be no proof, nor verification. When such is the case, one cannot say one's belief is correct and another's wrong, or one's is superior and another's inferior. One can be strong in one's own belief, but one has no right to force one's belief on some other. What is essential is that the belief should be consistent and satisfy the heart and gives a purpose and direction to life. There are so many theories about the universe and life apart from the scientific ones (even they are not confirmed, as there is no scope for verification, the key factor in the scientific method), but as they are all based on belief, one cannot claim one's own to be the right one. That is why the Australians have come to recognize that the aborigines have a right to their own system of belief regarding God and the universe and started paying respect to it. We have to say that tolerance is the basic requirement for a religion. Tolerance means tolerance not only towards the people of other beliefs, but also towards those who have no belief at all. For, some recognize the mystery of the universe and life, but do not subscribe to the conception of God, while some others completely reject the idea of mystery and god. One has the right to believe or not believe. What is more important is how one behaves in society, whether one, whatever one's belief or unbelief, understands others' needs and ideas and respects them. Intolerance indicates aggressiveness which is an antisocial trait. It is here most religions fail, so intelligent people should strive to overcome this tendency on the part of religions and inculcate tolerance among all people.

We must note another aspect of this tendency. Some religious people have a feeling of hostility to science, which they consider to be inimical to their beliefs. Nothing can be more wrong than that. Religion belongs to the world of belief and science to the world of fact. Both are different and there need be no opposition between the two. For example, Christians may follow the Biblical theory of creation as a part of their belief but should go by science in the world of fact. Dr. C.V. Raman, India's great scientist and Nobel Laureate's remark best exemplifies this. Hindus take a bath in a river or sea when an eclipse starts and again when it ends. Being a Hindu, Dr. Raman was coming out of the sea after his ablutions at the beginning of an eclipse, when another senior scientist noticed him and addressed him in surprise: "You, Dr. Raman, a great scientist observing a superstitious practice!" Dr. Raman replied, "That is science, and this is sentiment." There is nothing wrong in some scientists being Christians, and some being Muslims and so on.

Another serious allegation against religions in general is that they interfere in fields outside their purview. Religion being solely based on faith should not surely interfere in social, economic, political and other such matters where we must go by the conditions and facts of the situation. Those who occupy positions in the religious authority may express their personal opinions (like any other citizen they too have the right to express their opinions) but should take the precaution of stating clearly that they are such and never use their authority to pronounce on matters outside their field. But there are vested interests here who resist the slightest change, they should certainly be shown their place. Let us remind ourselves what Jesus Christ long ago said "Render unto Caesar the things that are Caesar's, and unto God the things that are God's."

Another practice that is objectionable has to be pointed out. While performing religious duties or attending religious or semi-religious functions one may don the attire prescribed by their religious tradition, but in day to day life one should not protrude their separate religious identity. Our beliefs may be different, but in all other matters we should be like any other citizen. The stress should be on common humanity.

This lengthy defense of religion in a book urging a scientific attitude may look odd, but this is necessary, because religion happens to be the cause of many serious conflicts in the world, as well as a victim of vicious attacks from the understanding. Religion must be given its proper place, but at the same time any disturbing or harmful consequences flowing from its misuse should be fought without hesitation. That is the only intelligent way in dealing with religion

Science, Tradition and Custom

Since tradition has usually been associated with religion, some science enthusiasts urge the total rejection of tradition too. One part of the rejection of the tradition is the rejection of ancient mythology and legend and contempt for it. Such people apply their 'scientific' minds to mythology and legend and take pains to prove how absurd and irrational all those stories are. But it does not really require a scientist to prove this, any child can easily point out the absurdities, crudities and mistakes of the mythological stories. But these absurdities and crudities do not detract much from the value of mythology and legend. Do we not find anachronisms, mistakes and absurdities in Shakespeare's plays? But do these plays suffer much on account of them? The peculiar thing we find is, nobody takes pains to disprove the stories of Shakespeare's plays and even the Greek and the Roman mythologies. Those that face hostility and cynicism are the Biblical, Hindu and other such mythologies because they are associated with living religions and so opposition to those religions extends to their mythologies and legends as well. And there is also an assumption that these mythologies contribute to faith in these religions, and so a religion can be weakened by attacking the mythology associated with it. But belief in mythology is not so essential for belief in religion, as these gentlemen assume. One example is there. When the Theory of evolution was first propounded there was a great shock to the minds of the faithful in the Western countries and consequently there was a reaction on their part to the discoveries of science and in some cases to science itself. But soon truth established itself (as it was bound to do). Now most Christians have come to accept the Theory of Evolution. Yet the Bible, even with the story of Adam and Eve, has not lost its appeal to the Christians.[31] Only ignorant people and simpletons may take the mythologies and legends literally. But the remedy is to dispel ignorance and educate the people and make them develop a scientific outlook. When people develop such an outlook they will never confuse between fact and fiction. That will be enough to guard against error and falsehood. But science is not all, we have seen. Poetic and philosophic approach is also needed to appreciate the value of mythologies and legends.

If we approach them in this way they offer a lot that we cannot but cherish. There might be a modicum of history or real life events in the makeup of mythology. (That is how we find some striking parallels in various mythologies). But during the passage of time they must have got distorted and exaggerated. In some of the books on psychology an illustration is given how the psychologists gathered in a conference reported widely differing versions of a fight between two persons that had been carefully planned and rehearsed, and was later enacted before the learned gathering.[32] When such is the case with even recent events, what should we say of those dim, distant historical beginnings when there were no reliable records except the credulous and fanciful minds of people who were slowly going through a process of civilization. Fact and fiction might have mingled together and, further, the aspirations, longings and dreams of the people might have got mixed up. A defeat might have been turned into a victory. Some of the personages of those legends might have become special centers of popular beliefs and dreams. A small adventurer might have been developed into a great hero.[33] Imaginative persons and poets might have worked up those tales and legends, and added to them their own stories of pure imagination and fancy.

Secondly, we see that poets, writers and preachers generally resort to metaphor and allegory to bring something abstract into the ken of the ordinary people. Many of the mythologies and legends reveal the metaphorical and allegorical significance, if properly studied. Not only ideas and ideals etc., of man, but also natural occurrences and phenomena are made into metaphors and allegories. The characters whether of metaphor or allegory once created begin to have a life of their own.[34] Not only that, they also give birth to offspring, have interrelations, conflicts and all. Thus, in the course of time fact, fiction, metaphor and allegory get mixed up, around which the aspirations, dreams and beliefs of the people get entwined and all blossom together into a rich world of mythology and legend. Poetry, art and philosophy (science too within limits) can together reveal what lies behind that world and then we find the greatest joy and delight, and even enlightenment in mythology and legend.[35] To the extent we find no emotional pleasure from them we can say we have lost the power of feeling itself to that extent. We are reminded of the words of Wordsworth

"—Great God: I'd rather be

A Pagan suckled in a creed outworn,

So might I, standing on this pleasant lea,

Have glimpses that would make me less forlorn;

Have sight of Proteus rising from the sea;

Or hear old Triton blow his wreathed horn"

A few words must be said about the customs, festivals and rituals handed over to us by tradition. Modern civilized man no longer finds any significance behind these customs, festivals etc. His life is totally alien to the life in which they sprang up. So, it is natural that they should appear empty to him and he tends to discard them. Let us remember that these customs, festivals, rituals etc., occupied a great deal of the life of man in the past. To the extent modern man has discarded the old customs, rituals etc., he has found a void which he has not been able to fill up with something worthwhile except with too much work, too much money-making and too much pleasure-seeking. Hence is the dissatisfaction and ennui man feels today at the height of his power and achievement.

For one thing, we see man does not do a thing simply, but does it in a particular way. Suppose somebody to whom we are closely attached dies: why should we go through all the funeral ceremonies and formalities when we know that the life is gone and there is nothing more to be done about it? We can simply call the undertaker and the undertaker along with his men comes and takes away the body in a truck and dumps it in a pit and covers it up, or burns it in an incinerator—everything simply and mechanically, and strictly in a practical way.[36] Can we be content with that? We want to linger on the memories of the departed, his remains too have an appeal to us and all these ceremonies and rituals lengthen those sad and sublime moments and thus give us solace and satisfaction, when our own mind and heart cannot provide them. Similarly, all the ceremonies and rituals associated with birth, marriage etc., also add special significance to those cherished moments and enrich them. From a strictly utilitarian point of view (which is what the rationalist point of view becomes in effect) even the system of marriage is unnecessary. If we proceed in this manner, we may do away with architecture—in what does the beauty of a building add to the primary purpose of providing shelter? We can extend the attitude to food and dress. If we proceed further in this way, even poetry and arts will have to go. Let us remind ourselves that man does not want to merely live. He wants to live beautifully, richly and well so that his whole personality finds fulfilment.

Just as man feels the need for arts, philosophy and religion, so too he feels the need for customs, ceremonies, festivals, rituals etc. That is why when we begin or accomplish something we like to celebrate the event. Why, even in a perfectly business meeting some form and ceremony is observed. When an event or function is such that it involves our sentiments and emotions, ceremony and ritual help in deriving the maximum emotional delight or satisfaction out of it. Even hippies who reject tradition and custom flock together, have their own congregations and festivals and have even developed their own customs and ritual. Knowing the need for ceremonies, festivals etc., even the communist governments, which suppressed religion to a great extent, evolved their own elaborate ceremonies and festivals which almost became imperative for the communist faithful. So if we give up the traditional customs, festivals etc., we have to create new ones in their place. But generally the artificially created ones lack the emotional and sentimental content which the traditional ones have. That is why some of the ceremonies and festivals imposed by authority disappear as soon as the compulsion is removed. In the case of hippies what holds them together is a negative factor and not a positive one. Such a bond cannot be long-lasting.

We have also to see why the traditional customs etc., have rich sentimental and emotional content. One of the most prominent characteristics of modern civilization is the speed and extent of communications. But surprisingly as physical communications have reached the highest efficiency, man has lost his own power of communication. Communication gaps have developed between man and man, and even between the members of a family, between father and son, between brother and brother. Even creative writers and artists are faced with the problem of communication. Hence is the search for exotic, complicated and totally new ways of expression. This has resulted in obscurity which is a common complaint against much modern art and literature. All this is because of the alienation of modern man from his own tradition and cultural heritage. That is why some of the writers and artists have turned back to primitive techniques and styles in order to recover some of the original spirit and inspiration.

Because of the alienation man has lost the capacity of sharing his feelings and experiences with others and equally of sharing others' feelings and experiences. The pace of civilization is such that man has become a cog in the wheel and finds little time to understand himself and realize himself. If he can manage to find a few calm moments and do some introspection he will realize that while he has his own individuality, he is also fundamentally a part of a wider entity, that is, society. To block the channels of his contact with society is thus to block the source of life. Here is the need for customs, festivals etc. They bring together individual men and make them share common feelings, memories and experiences. Suppose we are in a strange city. We feel like a fish out of water there. Suppose unexpectedly we come across another person whose ways of life are like our own, who eats like us, and dresses like us, we feel a great relief and joy. Similarly when we see thousands of others do something on a particular occasion just as we do, we forget our loneliness and feel one with all of them. We feel more so when a custom or festival we observe is observed all over the country. Realizing this, the modern totalitarian governments organize grand festivals, mammoth demonstrations and processions, mass athletics and activities so that the individual can come out of his narrow confines and feel himself a bigger and more powerful being. But these government-ordered festivals and ceremonies rarely touch the deeper cords of man. That is why a man experiences a sort of intoxication when he is part of the massive show, but once he is alone he feels deflated and dispirited.

Here the traditional customs, ceremonies etc., score over the ones imposed by authoritarian governments. They come naturally to us. (Really, to break with them requires a greater effort). They can easily bring people together. Further they have a long history, and if we trace them to their origin, we realize their significance and value too. Through these customs and festivals etc., we feel one not only with the people of our times, but also with the people who lived before us. We share their joys and sorrows, aspirations and beliefs and experiences. Thus, our existence is, as it were, extended to time immemorial and we feel the continuity of human life, and this gives a direction and meaning to our life. Hence is the value of mythology and legend, custom, ritual and festivals. If some people do not find any significance or value in them, it is only because they have not understood them properly. But this is not to advocate conformism. Blind acceptance and total rejection are equally wrong. There is much that is dead and decadent in the past. We must definitely reject what is reprehensible to our culture and civilization and what goes totally against our social and political norms and what revives only the evil and shameful past. We also find that a great portion of the ceremony and ritual was the conscious creation of the greedy priestly class purely with a selfish motive. There is no other value in it. We must definitely discard such ceremony and ritual. But let us not throw away the good and the beautiful along with the bad and the ugly. So, whatever we accept, we accept consciously and willingly. For this purpose we have to apply our intelligence to tradition and customs and understand them properly. (At the same time let us not make the mistake of judging tradition and custom solely by our present standards and ideological considerations).

Some of the traditional ceremonies, festivals etc., may have no relevance at all to modern life, even then they need not be given up, if only they serve to take us to our ancestors and those times, and thus add some excitement and interest to our own lives.

But this is not to deny the value of innovation, creativity and originality. We cannot be said to live fully without creating something in our own turn and adding our own contribution to culture and heritage. But the way is not by total rejection of the past. We must base our effort and achievement on whatever good and beautiful can be found in the past. (Let us not take this too literally. We cannot erect a new floor on an old and rotten building. The rotten structure must be demolished first, before a new building can be erected in its place. Yet we preserve an old building that has historical, cultural or sentimental value as a priceless treasure of our heritage. So we do not raze the old buildings and erect new ones in their place. We preserve whatever is valuable and build our own by their side. In building our own we often take ideas from the old and integrate them into the new. So it is hoped the readers will take it in the proper sense when it is said that we should build upon the past).

There are some people, of course, who cannot accept religion and do not find any value at all in tradition and custom. To them even sentiments and emotions are suspect. We cannot convince them, nor compel them to accept religion and tradition. We have already admitted that each man should be free to live his life as he likes, so long as he does not cause harm or suffering to others by his way of life. But at the same time, such persons cannot be considered in anyway superior to other people simply because they have rejected tradition and custom. It may indeed be a deficiency on their part. That they are leading successful lives without the necessity of tradition and custom is also no argument against the latter. Do not animals live without many of the things man needs and cherishes? (This should not be taken as equating atheists, nihilists and others with animals). But let them not claim the authority of science for their attitudes and ways of life. It has already been pointed out that it cannot be open mindedness if one refuses to recognize the needs and experiences of others. But the rationalists will be on firm ground if they attack superstition and positively harmful customs and practices. To repeat what has already been said, our acceptance of the past is conditional upon the acceptance of science.

The total rejection of religion and tradition is on par with the despoiling, disfiguring and even destruction of Nature and upsetting of ecological balance carried on in the name of science and technology. Man has now recognized where the blind pursuit of technology and civilization will lead to. It is really a result of misunderstanding science. So, we remind ourselves of the ancient Indian triple ideal of Satyam, Sivam, Sundaram (Truth, goodness and Beauty) which will not allow us to lose sight of our bearings.

Knowledge is responsibility

The reiteration of the ancient Indian motto of Satyam, Sivam, Sundaram takes us to a cardinal truth. Earlier in a note (NO. 17 Chapter IV Scientific Thinking, Section; The Value of Scientific Approach) we have seen that knowledge should also be considered a responsibility. Readers must have by now understood that though all along I have described the power of knowledge in the form of astonishing achievements of science and technology, the main thrust of my argument is that knowledge is a responsibility. Little children are not punished or treated the way adults are. It is because they do not know, we say. If at all we must blame, we blame their parents and hold them responsible. Similarly, an insane person is not considered responsible for his deeds, however violent they may be, because his mind is totally out of order. He is sent to an asylum and certainly not to a prison. (That is why some lawyers resort to the plea of temporary insanity to save their clients when there is no other way!). Also, we do not try animals and punish them according to law. (Of course we do come across such quixotic judgments now and then. They come more under the "Believe it or not" category).

All this shows that knowledge means responsibility. And also, that responsibility is commensurate with one's knowledge. The higher the knowledge, the higher the responsibility. In this connection it is interesting to learn about the ancient Hindu attitude towards knowledge. According to Hindu tradition the greatest importance is given to knowledge. In the Bhagavadgeeta the Lord says: " I am dearest to the knower and he too is dearest to me". No limits or restrictions are placed on the seeker of knowledge. In the Naasa Sukta of the Veda (the word 'Veda 'itself is derived from the root Vid to know). The seeker dares to question whether the Almighty himself knows all about the creation. But the knowledge referred to here is not the knowledge as we understand commonly. The knowledge that is mostly confined to the physical world is called Vignan, that is, science. The knowledge referred to above is called Gnan. It penetrates deep into man's inner self on the one hand, and on the other, extends up to the whole universe and concerns itself with the meaning and purpose of man's life on earth and his relationship with the rest of the creation. Such knowledge necessarily gives a perspective to man's vision and makes him humble, understanding and responsible. That is why the great ancient poet Bhartrihari says "When I knew nothing I was quite arrogant that I knew everything. Now that I know something I have come to realize I know almost nothing." When a man is humble, understanding and responsible his actions cannot but be good (and also beautiful). Thus we see once again the relevance of the ancient ideal of Satyam, Sivam, Sundaram.

Though Gnan and Vignan come under the same heading, the knowledge, there is actually no strict correspondence between the two. One may not know about what is called science, yet may be profound in one's gnan. The great Upanishadic seers of India, Gautama the Buddha, Adi Shankaracharya, Swami Vivekananda, Confucius and Lao Tse of China, Jesus Christ and Mohammad and most of the world's great philosophers such as Socrates, Spinoza, Kant, Scopenhauer etc., and also some of the great writers like Kalidasa, Shakespeare and Tolstoy, all these exemplify this point. Their hold on men's minds is far greater than that which any scientist can ever expect to have. They were all concerned with deeper and everlasting aspects of man's life and his future. That is why men of all ages have been looking to them for guidance and assurance. (But, simply because we have included some of the founders of religions in the list above, let us not confuse this gnan with religion. Religion is based primarily on faith and assurance, gnan often shakes up faith.)

However, we have to say that, though the two types of knowledge appear to be of different dimensions and directions, they are yet not opposed to each other, for fundamentally they are one and the same: the search for truth. So, these leaders may not have much scientific knowledge but their basic way of thinking cannot be irrational and illogical, or in other words unscientific. In so far as any of these great men showed irrationality anywhere, to that extent they exposed their own weak or dark spots. This warns us not to worship any person blindly, how so ever great he may be, and surrender our own thinking totally to him. Like the ancient seer already referred to we can certainly question the Almighty himself. (Of course, we must have the capacity to question. Mere ignorance cannot be our qualification. We must possess the basic quality of a seeker, eagerness to learn in all humility. That was why the ancient gurus never said "I am going to teach you gnan." They used to say "Let us explore together and seek truth."

The scientific revolution started with the exhilarating, or rather, intoxicating, idea that "Knowledge is power." Only towards the end of the last century the idea that "Knowledge is also freedom" began to take shape, for it was seen that as knowledge spread, many peoples all over the world began to throw away the shackles of subjection and fight for freedom from exploitation as well as from foreign domination.

What knowledge that is power (which is nothing but science and technology) can do has been all too evident to us. The mind-boggling achievements of science and technology, especially in the past century, seem to have reinforced the invincibility of the idea. That is how we see some of the scientists failing to realize that their discoveries and theories, however revolutionary and of far-reaching significance they may be, are yet a tiny meteor in the vast universe of knowledge which is yet to be discovered and which may not be discovered fully after all. They make arrogant assertions on man and God and what not. But it is also in the past century and now after two devastating world wars and increasing pollution of the environment, that an unease has begun to be felt by man and he has increasingly begun to ask whether science is really an unmixed blessing. Protest movements have sprung up on the premise that science is indeed half a curse. We have seen that knowledge leads to freedom. And that freedom is considered the greatest desirable thing for man for which any sacrifice is not too much. But we have now realized that freedom too has almost degenerated into license, corruption, chaos and cruelty to man, animal and environment.

Yes, science is itself no curse, but science without responsibility is a curse. So also, freedom itself is no curse, but freedom without responsibility is certainly a curse. How one would wish that modern man had started first with the idea that knowledge is responsibility, then only freedom and then only power instead of the way he has really done. Thus, we come round to our point that the greater the power, the greater the responsibility. But the knowledge that is power cannot give the idea of responsibility. It is gnan, the other kind of knowledge that stresses that idea. So, must a great scientist be also a great gnani or philosopher, one may ask. Not necessarily. It is enough if he has the minimum necessary basic knowledge that is called gnan. He should not be totally immersed in his own researches and discoveries. He should know fully the consequences of his discoveries and theories. He should realize that he is only a part of a wide, vast world and know what is happening around him. He should consciously and willingly fulfill the minimum necessary duties as part of that world. He should be humble and understanding.

We come to the other aspect of this matter. We have seen that knowledge entails responsibility, but it is equally true that responsibility presupposes knowledge. There can be no responsibility without knowledge. That is why we do not entrust children or ignorant men with any responsibility. In offices too one is entrusted with higher and higher responsibilities as one gains experience (which is really an extension of knowledge). But many people fear responsibility. So, they shut their eyes on what is going on around or refuse to acquire further knowledge so that they can limit their responsibility to the utmost minimum. That is wrong. We can indeed call such an attitude inhuman, for having been invested with mind it is man's basic responsibility to see, observe and think and then act according to that knowledge. In other words, knowledge is man's responsibility and knowledge is a responsibility too.

Thus, in the end we realize the validity of the basic principle of Hindutva "Dharmo rakshati rakshitah" which means if you protect dharma, dharma will protect you. Dharma is not religion as is misunderstood in some quarters. Dharma is that which sustains not only the humanity but also the whole creation. It means the realization that we are a part of the whole and the awareness of our responsibility not to disturb or destroy the relationships between us and the rest of the universe in any way, but to sustain it and strengthen it by all means at our disposal. When we are fully aware of that responsibility we cannot but seek knowledge in all humility and cannot but put that knowledge in the service of not only mankind but all animals, plants and trees, rivers, oceans and mountains, indeed the whole universe.

A Note on Patriotism

A few words must be said about patriotism which has become suspect in the eyes of some people. In this age of science, especially after the loosening hold of traditional beliefs and customs and the spread of cosmopolitanism, a class of people have come up who look down upon all such things as patriotism, love of one's own language, love of one's religion etc., as petty and narrow-minded things unsuited to the age. Some even proclaim that patriotism conceals crass stupidity.

Let us first take up this question. Is all patriotism invariably stupid? Was there no difference between the patriotism of Hitler and that of Gandhiji? Hitler too loved his country. He strove for the glory of Deutschland. Not only did he exterminate six million Jews, but also plunged the whole world into the most disastrous war. Thus, the patriotism of Hitler in the end resulted in incalculable harm to his own country. Surely, such patriotism must be condemned and fought. But Gandhiji loved even his enemy. That was why even after independence India continued to associate with her former master. In the very first year of independence, when Pakistan instigated and supported hordes overran Kashmir, the then Government of India wanted to hold back an amount due to Pakistan, as a retaliatory measure. But Gandhiji compelled the Government to deliver to Pakistan what was her due. Was Gandhiji's patriotism harmful to the country and the world? In fact, Gandhiji's patriotism itself laid the foundations of universalism. Will it not be foolish and unscientific too (for science never overlooks facts and conditions) if we do not take all this into account, but simply condemn patriotism wholesale?

To come back to our cosmopolitans: They say that it is nationalism that creates conflicts between countries and thus leads to war. One must admit the truth of this to some extent, because history gives us many instances to the effect. But we should look deeper into the matter. Then we shall find something even behind nationalism. There is some truth in the materialist point of view that material circumstances give rise to or determine man's ideas. Behind nationalism we find economic factors—other factors too are there, but economic factors are more important. These condition to a large extent the functioning of the political institutions. We have not yet arrived at such a stage that these institutions of the various countries can be harmonized and adjusted to each other so that there may be no friction. That is why we have conflicts. These are predominantly conflicts of economic interests. They come out in the form of aggressive nationalism, the cause of tension, confusion and suffering in the world. But we cannot simply suppress or make people give up their aggressive nationalism without changing the economic and financial institutions of the nations. That is certainly a Herculean task. But meanwhile we should at least see that the aggressive type of nationalism is held in leash.

The nationalism just mentioned is only one side of the coin. There is the other side too. If we say that the aggressive nationalism of Germans, Italians, and the Japanese led to the Second World War, we should also say that it was the intense nationalism of the peoples of Russia, England and other countries that saved them from being overrun by the fascist hordes. It was the patriotism of the Russian people that was appealed to, and that worked a miracle when that country was invaded in the nineteenth century by Napoleon and again in the twentieth by Hitler. It was patriotism again that made a small nation, Vietnam, so heroic and made her perform unheard of sacrifices and put up such a stiff fight against the Number One Super Power of the world. Patriotism is something that transforms a clod of earth into a ball of fire. We cannot explain it in strictly material terms. We have admitted that the economic factors are very important, but they are not everything. There are other factors too. And at times they may overrule the economic factors. If the latter only were the deciding ones why should any body sacrifice himself for the nation? If at all he must sacrifice, he must sacrifice others for his own benefit. Secondly, patriotism means love of one's country. And country does not mean merely the land, the mountains, rivers forests etc.,[37] but mainly the people living in it. So patriotism means intense fellow-feeling for the people on one's own land. Such a feeling will counteract the divisive and destructive tendencies within the nation, and when patriotism fires the nation, huge tasks of national reconstruction can be undertaken and successfully accomplished, so that inequalities can be reduced and injustices removed. Only when there is patriotic zeal will people be prepared to sacrifice and forget their narrow self-interest and rush to the help of their less fortunate brothers. It does not mean that patriotism suddenly transforms a backward country into a great one. But it will strengthen and accelerate the pace of that transformation.

Thus, from a nation's internal point of view patriotism or nationalism is a great constructive force.

But patriotism too has certain limitations. It is not something against material circumstances. It rises in them and goes beyond them. It is no substitute for food, health and shelter. When people are hungry and in misery, preaching patriotism to them is the worst hypocrisy. Patriotism also cannot work in an atmosphere of apathy and despair. The people must have a sense of belonging. They must have at least hope for the future. The people of Vietnam did not have a standard of life that could be compared with that of Americans, but they had a sense of belonging, a conviction that they had a share in the fortunes of their country. That was why they fought so gloriously. Similarly, the people of the Soviet Union might have suffered much under Stalin's rule. Yet they had the awareness that the country was theirs, the government was theirs, and despite its obvious faults it was doing something for them. They felt they had a stake in the freedom of the country. That was why they fought heroically even though their homes and farms and factories were destroyed. But it is also an undeniable fact that patriotism has an emotional appeal. It often makes the people forget even their misery. So dictators, tyrants and unscrupulous politicians, knowing the appeal of patriotism, make use of it to the maximum extent. In order to turn away the peoples' attention from the difficulties and disasters at home they rouse their anger against real or imagined foes. But because dictators and such others make use of patriotism, we need not condemn it totally. The dictators and others exploit the ignorance of the people who cannot distinguish between truth and falsehood, between the genuine variety of patriotism and the perversion of it. The remedy is not the condemnation of patriotism, but the spread of knowledge.

Not taking all this into consideration, the cosmopolitans want us in the name of internationalism to give up our languages, our culture, our national, religious and even family loyalties. What is this internationalism? What is its shape and function? How can it be realized? But we do not get clear-cut answers. Peoples of many backward countries (who form the majority of the population of the world) have not yet arrived at a stage of true nationalism. They have not yet realized what their own culture is. Yet these cosmopolitans want them to give up their national culture. Are nationalism and internationalism absolute opposites? Does universal culture demand the destruction of national cultures?

In the Bible it is said that he who cannot love his brother on the earth cannot love the unseen in heaven. So we have to really doubt the internationalism of those who say they love the whole of humanity, but cannot love their own fellowmen in their native country. We cannot take at its face value the universal culture of persons who reject their own national culture.

The truth is, desire for self-advancement, love of one's own kith and kin, love of one's own group or region, love of one's country and love of humanity are all loyalties at different levels in an ascending order. They can co-exist at their various levels. If one looks after one's family it does not mean that one has to hate others. If one loves one's country it does not follow inevitably that one hates other countries. Conversely, we can say if one loves one's country it does not mean that one should give up loving one's own family. One can love humanity while loving one's own country, one's own region, and one's own family. It is only when the higher loyalty really demands it, one may have to sacrifice the lower one. If one's country is in danger, one must be prepared to sacrifice anything—even one's life—for the sake of the country. If one's country commits aggression against another, one should have the courage and strength to stand up against one's own country's policy.

Thus, there is no real conflict between true love of one's own good and true nationalism and true internationalism. The conflict is between the wrong manifestations of various loyalties. So normally the higher loyalty should not demand the suppression or sacrifice of the loyalties at the lower levels without a definite purpose. In the name of the state Hitler and Mussolini suppressed individual freedom. Such a 'higher' loyalty cannot really be a higher one. So what we need, as pointed out in the political science textbooks, is harmonizing and right ordering of loyalties.[38]

Just as we have seen that it is wrong to condemn nationalism or any other loyalty wholesale simply because there are some harmful and evil manifestations of it, so also we should not go to the other extreme and justify each and every loyalty. For, some loyalties like those of caste, creed, tribe and race are indefensible and should be rooted out. Once upon a time it used to be said 'Right or wrong, my country'. Now we have 'Right or wrong, my fellow student, worker or professional' and so on. Just as the former attitude is considered totally wrong and pernicious, these narrow loyalties too should be considered in the same way. Whatever loyalty that is sought to justify a wrong is reprehensible and should be eradicated. But our approach should not be merely negative. We should not be content with fighting against such loyalties, we should actively encourage and cultivate beneficial loyalties in place of the former.

So what we require is intelligence to discern and separate the good from the bad. Here political science has a great role to play. It should help us in understanding the background and genesis of each type of loyalty, what effect it has on the individuals concerned and on society and whether it harmonizes with other loyalties and helps the right ordering of them or whether it conflicts with others and creates disorder and suffering. We can gather all the facts by applying the scientific approach to our social and political matters, and such knowledge will help us in regulating and ordering our loyalties. It tells us the limits beyond which a loyalty (including patriotism) loses its positive and beneficial quality and assumes a negative and harmful one. We can thus realize that these loyalties are—as has already been pointed out—a series of ascending steps that take us higher and higher towards real humanity. A man who can range through all these loyalties freely and without conflict may be considered the perfect man. Some people may not have the necessary vision or temperament or strength to reach out to the wider loyalties. Some may be able to think only of their families. Some people can think only of their region. But there should be no objection if these loyalties are not negative and if they fit into the harmonious ordering of loyalties of the whole nation. But our goal should be that maximum number of people reach out to the widest number of loyalties.

It has already been pointed out that we have not yet reached a truly international stage. Even now freedom is not a reality to many peoples. When life within nations becomes free and harmonious we are ready for the higher stage of internationalism. When a man has taken all the steps to nationalism he can easily take the next higher step. So too a whole people. Let us harness the powerful force of patriotism to the vast tasks of national reconstruction and removal of inequality and injustice. That should be our immediate aim.

True patriotism is, indeed, the preliminary step to internationalism.[39] Let science help us in distinguishing the true patriotism from the false one. Whoever thinks that he has rejected patriotism altogether and hence is a scientific man is nothing of the sort.

To stress one point before closing this note, even true internationalism does not mean the disappearance of different nations, language, cultures etc. It only means harmonious relationships between different nations and integration of their activities at a higher level. Those who dream of the ideal one humanity, one nation, one language, one culture etc. live in a false world. They have not understood man properly. If ever such an ideal were to be realized that would indeed be the end of man as man.

Despite all that I have written about patriotism, I strongly condemn jingoism, chauvinism and other such vicious things. Just as the attitude 'My country, right or wrong' is reprehensible, so also is the extreme obsession with one's country's great past, great cultural heritage etc. However great and glorious one's country's achievement in the past might be, what we are now, what we are going to do, how we are going to incorporate the best and precious of our past in our present lives and what we ourselves are contributing to make our heritage a continuous, living and dynamic one, and what foundations we are lying for the future—this is all that matters. We must live in the present and move forward and not backwards. If we have the sense and strength to carry the best of our tradition and cultural heritage with us we shall be all the more richer and our future too will be more glorious than even before.

Further, one does not love one's mother because she is a high-born lady, or highly educated and cultured lady, or a rich and prosperous lady. One loves one's mother, be she rich or poor, educated or illiterate. I may be proud of the fact that I was born in India, but if I were born in a very poor country, a dreary desert or a dense forest all around and which has no history, culture and literature worth speaking of, I would still love that country alone, and my duty too would primarily be towards—'my poor and backward motherland'"

The great tradition and heritage of our country or its present affluence and prosperity should indeed make us more humble, for all that wealth either of the past or of the present, only places responsibility on us. We should strive our utmost to share our wealth (culture or otherwise) with our fellow men in other countries which are less fortunate than ours.

Intelligence For Full Life

Thus, while applying the scientific approach to our social and political matters, we should never lose sight of its limitations too. For example, the scientist who dissects the rose and tells us so many facts about it should not deny the need for and the existence of the poet, the artist or the philosopher. At the same time the latter should not look down upon the scientist, because he disfigured the beautiful rose and thrust the cold knife into its heart. The scientist by his dissections and studies has helped us in growing more beautiful and healthier roses in abundance and also in richer variety. Thus, science really helps us in the appreciation and enjoyment of beauty. Let us also not forget the fact that science has produced new arts of its own like photography and cinema and at the same time, it has diversified and, in a way, enriched the old arts like painting and architecture. It is science that has rescued and preserved the great master pieces of art, architecture and literature. It is again science that has made it possible for more men to come to know and enjoy the glorious treasures of art and literature. Thus, we can say that but for science, man's (meaning, the whole mankind's) enjoyment of art and literature would be far more restricted. Not only this, but science also helps rid religion of much of its dross and makes it brighter and purer.

Indeed, science contributes to the richer life of man, helps him to realize his own personality to the maximum extent. Keeping the limitations in mind, we can yet say that science is always a blessing unless we believe knowledge is evil and ignorance is bliss.

This long chapter is only to stress the fact that man is a myriad-faceted multi-colored personality. All the various aspects must be nurtured and developed for him to realize himself fully. Everybody has potentialities for development, but few understand this truth, that is the pity of it!

But before I close this section I should like to add two more items to the list of qualifications necessary for a full man. They are the love of the animal world and Nature. The latter of course includes the former, but has to be mentioned separately to stress the importance of the former in its own right. This is not the place for explaining at length the necessity for the love of animals and Nature. It is enough if we understand that they indicate the sensibility and the breadth and depth of the vision of man. Love is more than mere kindness. It implies a deeper affinity. It takes one to the very fountain springs of life as it were. A man who feels that deeper affinity with Nature including the animal world brings a refreshing approach to man's own problems. He cannot be a party to the meaningless strife and cruelty that is rampant in the world. We can also say that the senseless cruelty to animals and the reckless destruction of nature have brutalized man himself to an unusual degree and we are reaping its horrible consequences all around us.[40]

Finally, What is Intelligence after all?

There is a joke in Telugu (the writer's mother tongue). After listening to the musical narration of Ramayana, the story of Rama and his wife, Sita a man was said to have asked, "What was Sita to Rama?"

The question posed in the heading above may raise many a quizzical smile. The whole burden of this book is about intelligence. Is not the question now absurd? But there is some reason for putting that question, for intelligence is not an entity, not a concrete term. It is only an activity from the results of which we can recognize its existence. In the simplest terms it is awareness of oneself and one's surroundings. But it is also not something given once and for all. Like a tiny seed growing into a huge banyan tree, so also it started with a few elements, evolved with life and now with man encompasses the whole world in all directions and in all fields, now even spreading to worlds beyond. As said above, it is an active process. From the results we go to the process and from the process to the results and again to the process, in ever widening circles.

And intelligence is not of one kind. Like the same energy functioning as heat, light, sound, x-rays and so on intelligence too is observed in many forms. There is an exploitative kind which always is on the lookout for an opportunity and when it finds one it makes use of it to the utmost. This can be seen in businessmen, capitalists, entrepreneurs and others. There is the organizational variety which is found in political leaders, social leaders, military leaders and such others. Then there is the creative intelligence manifested in poets, writers, artists, architects, music composers etc., and the enquiring intelligence is represented by scientists, explorers and others. And then there is the philosophical and spiritual kind which concerns itself with the higher things of life. It aims at synthesis at higher and still higher levels. All these forms of intelligence are not as if in airtight compartments. They are interconnected. A doctor or a scientist or an engineer may also be a good writer or artist or musician. A capitalist, for example, if he is to be successful should not only be able to find out and seize opportunities, but also have knowledge about them and the right way to use them Besides he too must have ability to organize resources to achieve his end. The political and social leaders and others should have not only the organizational ability, but also sufficient knowledge about the things they deal with. Some people may be confined to only one or two fields, but a man's worth is proved by the fields he covers in his sweep and the higher and higher levels he reaches. Thus intelligent activity means on the one side acting to protect oneself, one's species and, further, the surrounding world and on the other side recognizing that man's aim is not just to live, but understanding his unlimited and multifarious abilities and as a consequence his enormous responsibilities too. The difference between intellect and intelligence (they are not against each other, they come from the same source) should be noted. A man of great intellect may not have a good life proportionate to his great intellect. A man of average intellect may have a successful life and earn the appreciation of his friends and neighbors. Gandhi and Nelson Mandela are good examples.

All creatures from the lowest worm to the biggest animals can be called intelligent in so far as they make good of their lives. But we cannot think of intellect in relation to them. Intellect is the exclusive trait of man. Intelligence covers science, arts, philosophy, religion, indeed, everything connected with man's life.

So what is now called I.Q. (Intelligence Quotient) should be called Intellect Quotient. What is being said to be Artificial Intelligence should be called Artificial Intellect. Robots may excel man thousands of times in the future but they can never have any intelligence. They can never displace man.

NOTES

Chapter I: Introductory

1. The cost of the First World War estimated to be $ 196.5 billion (corrected to the 1990 value of the dollar.)
2. The cost of the Second World War was estimated to be $2091 billion (corrected to the 1990 value of the dollar.)
3. All these excerpts are from an article titled 'The Special Session on Disarmament' by Punyapriya Das Gupta, published in the Indian Express (Vijayawada Edition) dated May 15, 1978.

Chapter II: Intelligence in Action

4. Only a very sketchy outline is attempted here. Naturally nothing has been said here about the nomadic stage. But that does not come in the way of understanding the nature and function of intelligence. There are exceptions, of course. For example, the phenomenon of lemmings, an Arctic variety of rodents, committing mass suicide now and then has defied scientific explanation so far.
5. In India too in the Northeast we hear of similar actions on the part of some species of birds. We said that there is no thought about the future in animals. But ants do store food for the future.
6. Of course in certain species of birds and animals (very few) the companionship is for life.
7. We must not make the mistake of equating the primitive

savages with the savages of recent times. The latter-day savages have had already thousands of years of tradition, stabilized and stylized forms of social organization, elaborate rituals and customs etc.

8. That is why tools and implements are strictly utilitarian in construction. They are generally standardized. Only the non-essential parts, the handle, hilt or sheath, allow scope for fanciful decoration.

9. I seem to be contradicting my own earlier statement that by applying his intelligence man freed himself from absolute dependence on Nature. Definitely the civilized man was not as utterly at the mercy of Nature as animals were, or even as the primitive man was. He was able to exploit Nature's bounty to the maximum. Yet he could take what Nature gave him and could not force anything out of her as the man in the scientific age is able to do, as we shall see presently. He ploughed the land, watered it, and sowed the seeds. The rest depended on Nature and good fortune.

Chapter III: Thinking

10. The term, common sense, is however, taken in a positive way and is thought to be sound enough for ordinary life. So here after I substitute the term 'ordinary thinking' for 'common sense thinking.'

11. But it is also a fact that through language and literature in the widest sense—now we must add cinema, radio and television too—the wider society has an influence on the individual even from the early stages and competes with closer factors like family, friends, and community.

12. I have gone a little out of the way and discussed the relationship between the individual and society more elaborately than is required here, because such an understanding of the relationship will form a basic postulate in the subsequent discussion.

Chapter IV: Scientific Thinking

13. *A.E.Mander: Clearer Thinking. The Thinker's Library series No.57* Published by Watts & Co., London, pages 50—51. A Note: Some modern developments in science, especially the quantum theory and the uncertainty principles seem to cast a doubt on the validity of these fundamental principles. But the quantum theory and the uncertainty principle relate only to the micro world of atoms. For all practical purposes, as far as man's physical life is concerned, the principles stated above can be considered fundamental.

14. This should not be taken to mean that a scientist can create a system of his own and impose it on Nature. His system will be scientific only if it corresponds to the system in Nature.

15. Generally the term 'theory' is used only when it covers a wide class of facts, for example, the Theory of Evolution. When the scope is limited and confined to a particular class of facts, the scientist contents himself with the term 'findings', which means generalizations or general statements arrived at by the process described above.

16. There was one striking example in recent times: Hitler's Germany was remarkable both for her scientific and technological achievement and extremes of inhuman barbarity.

17. I should add "Knowledge is responsibility" also. Without responsibility freedom and power become pernicious. This aspect is dealt with in the subsequent pages of this book.

V: The Necessary Corollary of Thinking: Planning

18. Total planning is something more than full planning: the latter means planning for the whole society, but the former means planning not only for the whole society but also for all the aspects of society—those aspects too that the state has no direct concern with.

19. This aspect has been dealt with in some detail in the author's other book : *An Exposé of Marxism.*

VI: Limitations of Scientific Thinking

20. In this connection, the readers are referred to C.G.Jung's autobiographical work, Memories, Dreams, Reflections (The Fontana Library Theology and Philosophy—Collins 1972), particularly Chapter V Sigmund Freud. They will find plenty of proof for the statement made above.
21. There is a story to the effect by name "The Law of Life" by Jack London.
22. Buddha.
23. Emperor Ashoka
24. Jesus Christ.
25. Prophet Mohammed.
26. Mahatma Gandhi.
27. The great South Indian Music Composer.
28. It has elsewhere been remarked that even if Darwin had not been born, the Theory of Evolution would have been discovered sooner or later and the reason for the assumption has also been given. (please refer to Chapter IV) but geniuses are still inexplicable,. Especially in fields where creativity is required. There is no certainty and inevitability about great achievement. We should not go to the length of saying that great poets, artists and others are totally unrelated to time and circumstance, but it is certain they cannot be made to order. This explains why the Soviet Union which carried away the largest number of gold metals in the Olympics (games and sports is a field where training and determination can achieve a lot) and had also excelled in the fields of science and technology lagged behind in the matter of creative arts and literature. Even the statement above about Darwin and the Theory of Evolution must be qualified. it is generally agreed that the formulation of the working hypothesis and the final theory partake the character of creative thinking.

Such creative thinking cannot be had by everybody by mere training and practice. So some people can never become scientists. Yet it is also a fact that this kind of thinking can be cultivated and developed with a fair degree of certainty. This is proved by the achievements of science in the twentieth century. We have now, not tens of hundreds, but tens of thousands of scientists who can be said to be exercising such creative thinking. But the fundamental fact of "creativity" remains. For example, in the field of literature whereas formerly there used to be only a few score of short-story writers, now we have thousands of them. Yet the proportion of short-story writers to the total population is small, proving the fact of creativity. But let us not make an unnecessary mystery of it. There are levels of creativity. For example, deducing the conclusion from the premises of a syllogism is a tiny act of creativity, but we should remind ourselves that to the primitive man even this act was a very difficult step which he was able to make only over thousands of years. But nowadays most people can rise to a still higher level than that exemplified by the conclusion of a syllogism. If facts regarding, say, a political problem with the condition that it (the problem) does not involve sentiments or loyalties, are placed before the public in a systematic manner they can draw the necessary conclusions. We can also affirm with certainty that with the advance of education and culture most people rise to a higher level of creativity than has ever been possible, for, we realize by now, creativity is fundamentally a characteristic of intelligence. But when we rise higher and higher the certainty about creativity at those levels diminishes gradually. When we come to such theories as those that comprehend the whole universe and give a new turn to the thinking of mankind, for example, Newton's theories, Max Planck's Quantum Theory, Einstein's Theory of Relativity we are not so sure. They are flashes of genius which cannot be made to order. (In this connection the readers are referred to the article on 'The Mystery of Human Wisdom' by Dr. Jagjit Singh in the January 76 issue of SPAN published by the United States Information Service, New Delhi.)

VII: Beyond Science

29. This aspect must be studied deep. The environment or the external circumstances have no effect on the evolution process. THE HORSE IN THE DESERT DID NOT EVOLVE AS A CAMEL. The horse is a horse, a camel is a camel. The predator and the prey, the tiger and the deer have evolved in the same forest. Not only they, but also elephants, giraffes, zebras and thousands of other creatures, big, small and minute thrive in the same forest. If you go to the depths of oceans it is a whole mighty world of creatures. All the species on the planet are born with the genes necessary to make them fit to face the environment in which they are born. Once life is born external forces do start to take affect. Take any species of the millions of creatures in the world and study its structure and its activity you will be filled with wonder when you ask 'How' and 'Why'. It is an everlasting and never-ending mystery. The mind is our greatest possession. With it we have been constantly expanding the area of light around us. But, as we have just said, the mystery is endless. So let us carry on our inquiry with humility and an open mind.

30. Under Stalin 62 Million people died, while under Mao 35 million died as noted by K. Ashok Vardhan Shetty in When Man Exterminates Man published in The Hindu, Chennai, Hyderabad dated 16-9-2001.

31. To give another example: Milton's Paradise Lost is acclaimed by one and all as a great classic. It can be appreciated even by non—Christians and unbelievers. Yet if one proceeds to read it with the idea always in mind that the story and characters are all mere nonsense and that one is concerned only with the literary aspect of it then one will miss almost all the beauty and grandeur of the book. So in

order to appreciate its full beauty and excellence, one has to be prepared not merely for 'a willing suspension of disbelief'; but also for sharing the spirit of the book to some extent.

32. "At a Psychology Congress held at Gottingen a clown suddenly burst into the Congress hall closely pursued by a Negro. The Negro caught him, leapt upon him and bore him to the floor, when a fight ensued, which was ended by a pistol shot, after which the clown got up and rushed out of the room, still closely pursued by the Negro. The whole scene which had been carefully rehearsed and photographed in advance, took less than twenty seconds. The president then informed the Congress that judicial proceedings might have to be taken and asked each member to write a report stating exactly what had happened. Forty reports were sent in. Of these, one only contained less than twenty per cent of mistakes in regard to the principal facts; fourteen contained from twenty per cent to forty per cent mistakes, thirteen contained more than fifty per cent mistakes. In twenty—four, ten per cent of the details recorded were pure inventions. In short, ten per cent of the details recorded were pure inventions. In short, ten of the accounts were quite false, ranking as myths and legends, twenty—four were half legendary, and six only were even approximately exact". From Public Opinion, by Walter Lippmann as quoted by C.E.M. Joad in his book The Mind and its Workings.

33. An English writer wrote a book The Ballad and the Source. In it the writer points out that the source of a ballad may be not so great or noble, or even may be fiction, but that does not deprive the ballad of its value. It has to be treated as a separate and inspiring peace of vocal literature shared by the whole community.

34. An English writer wrote a book The Ballad and the Source. In it the writer points out that the source of a ballad may be not so great or noble, or even may be fiction, but that does not deprive the ballad of its value. It has to be treated as a

separate and inspiring peace of vocal literature shared by the whole community.

35. Some do not understand this and they approach mythology and legend standing on their heads, as it were. They parade their knowledge of social anthropology and cultural anthropology and such things and use them as weapons to tear mythology and legend to pieces. But if at all we apply social anthropology and cultural anthropology to mythology and legend it can only be to get whatever knowledge of history and development of human society from them and not to understand their value and beauty. The latter course would be like dissecting mother's body to understand mother's love.

36. Readers are, in this connection, referred to *Brave New World* by Aldous Huxley.

37. But the geographical factors—the hills, the rivers and streams, trees and meadows—also form an integral part of patriotism. Apart from the role they play in our economies we cannot overlook the fact that they have an abiding influence on our literature, arts, history and cultural heritage and they also enter our own mental and aesthetic make-up. That is why when people are transplanted from one environment to another, they feel restless and unhappy till they accustom themselves to the new environment. A desert-dweller in a great city would continue to long for the barren, burning desert. It is also a fact that some people, perhaps owing to some personal circumstances or some peculiarities in their mental and emotional make-up prefer a new environment and are happy there. Generally speaking, it is unwise to minimize the importance of geographical factors and concentrate attention only on the people, as some so-called progressives do.

38. We can rather put it in this way. Self-respect, love for one's own family, love for one's kith and kin and friends, love of one's own village or town, region, state and country, love of

the whole humanity are after all the same human values and sentiments operating at different levels.

39. This is not to suggest that we need not concern ourselves with internationalism as yet. While working for national reconstruction we have to act quickly on the international plane too, to remove the dangers that face humanity. The armament race and the cold war make such action urgent. Besides, the oil crisis, the food problem, monetary crisis, the problem of pollution etc., have forced us to think of the whole world as a unit. Above all man's intelligence is such that it can operate beyond the immediate material circumstances. We need not wait till conditions turn favorable to us. We can foresee and create the necessary conditions.

40. The love one has for one's pet or pets is not the same thing as the love for animals. The former is only a physical craving or personal need. Even criminals love their pets. Only large-hearted men love animals as animals. The love of animals stressed here rises above mere fondness and even kindness, it makes us see the problem of existence from the point of view of animals and makes us take the active steps to help them live their own lives well. It will not surely let us be content with occasional showy acts of 'kindness to animals.'

About the Author

Vaasamoorti, Varanasi Satyanarayana Murthy, has written ten novels, several short stories, general books and books for children, two of which were translated into other languages including Russian.

Vaasamoorti was born in a village on the banks of river Godavari. He had to discontinue his college studies due to a long crippling bone disease. After passing Hindi examinations he started his career as a Hindi teacher in a high school in Amalapuram, in Andhra Pradesh. Still later he appeared privately for Intermediate, BA in Economics, MA in English Language and Literature. In 1966, he joined the Department of English in S.K.B.R. college in Amalapuram, where he retired and continued to work on his books, novels and articles.

He started his literary career with an article in English, An Artificial Language in My india, a weekly from Bangaluru. His English works are Here and Beyond, a novel, The Language Revolution, dealing with the language situation in India, Marxism, Relevance and Practice, a critique of Marxism, Goodness and Good Manners and Thinking the Right Way.

He has wide-ranging interests. He started a film society and a science forum besides attending to his activities. He was associated with the consumer protection movement for some time and has been a keen lover of animals and the environment. He served as Editorial Assistant for an illustrated weekly for 11 years.

www.ingramcontent.com/pod-product-compliance
Lightning Source LLC
Chambersburg PA
CBHW071524150726
48000CB00002B/675